Train Your Empathy:

How to Cultivate the Single Most Important Relationship Skill

By Patrick King
Social Interaction and Conversation Coach at
www.PatrickKingConsulting.com

Table of Contents

CHAPTER 1: UNDERSTANDING EMPATHY AND WHY WE NEED IT — 7

THE NEUROBIOLOGY OF EMPATHY — 7
WHAT EMPATHY IS — 10
WHAT EMPATHY ISN'T — 12
THE THREE TYPES OF EMPATHY — 15
COMPASSION—A BALANCING ACT — 24

CHAPTER 2: HOW TO DISCOVER AND FLEX YOUR EMPATHY MUSCLES — 29

WHY READING MAKES YOU MORE EMPATHIC — 29
BECOME EMOTIONALLY LITERATE BY LABELING — 40

CHAPTER 3: ACCOUNTING FOR BIAS, PREJUDICE, EGO, AND PERSPECTIVE — 61

ROOT OUT BIAS AND PREJUDICE — 61
HOW TO TACKLE YOUR OWN BIASES AND PREJUDICE — 67
COMPASSION—ON THE OTHER PERSON'S TERMS — 71
THE FINE ART OF PERSPECTIVE-TAKING — 74
TWO ESSENTIAL INGREDIENTS FOR WALKING IN ANOTHER'S SHOES — 79
PERSPECTIVE-TAKING, STEP BY STEP — 81

CHAPTER 4: LISTENING IS EMPATHY IN ACTION — 91

DON'T JUST LISTEN ACTIVELY, LISTEN EMPATHICALLY	**91**
LISTENING IS ACTIVE!	**99**
THE BODY CAN LISTEN, TOO	**105**

CHAPTER 5: INJECTING EMPATHY INTO DAILY LIFE — 117

BE STILL AND REFLECT	**117**
BE CURIOUS	**130**
KEEP THE SPARK OF CURIOSITY ALIVE	**139**
RANDOM ACTS OF KINDNESS	**145**

CHAPTER 6: EMPATHIC COMMUNICATION IS THE ULTIMATE GOAL — 155

THE POWER OF EMPATHIC STATEMENTS	**155**
WHAT TO SAY, WHAT NOT TO SAY	**156**
AN EMPATHIC STATEMENT FORMULA	**165**
NONVIOLENT COMMUNICATION/NVC	**169**
HOW TO BE ASSERTIVE AND EMPATHIC	**184**
THE EMPATHIC COMMUNICATION TOOLKIT FOR HANDLING CONFLICT	**191**

SUMMARY GUIDE — 199

Chapter 1: Understanding Empathy and Why We Need It

The Neurobiology of Empathy

Empathy is the only human superpower—it can shrink distance, cut through social and power hierarchies, transcend differences, and provoke political and social change.

— *Elizabeth Thomas*

Empathy is a beautiful thing. When we have empathy, our world becomes bigger because we are able to share in the worlds of others and feel the satisfaction of knowing that they can see into our own. Empathy brings depth and meaning to our relationships—all kinds of relationships— and helps us smooth over conflict and misunderstanding.

Empathy is not just for the sake of others, though; if we develop empathy in ourselves, we can't help but find that we have more of it for ourselves. Empathy allows us to be more creative, more resilient, and more innovative when it comes to solving problems. With empathy, we become more self-compassionate, self-aware, and fully rounded individuals.

But while everyone can agree that empathy is great, the unfortunate truth is that we are rapidly becoming a world that has forgotten what it means to walk in someone else's shoes. A now notorious study conducted from 1979 to 2009 (Konrath et al., 2010) found that people's overall empathy scores dropped an astonishing forty-eight percent—and this is not including the last decade of drastically increased social media narcissism, political division, and cultural isolation.

Empathy is simply the ability to take on the perspective of someone else.

It means being able to see that your beliefs and biases are not objective reality, but merely a lens through which you view objective reality—and that everyone has *their* own lens, too. Empathy is the social, familial, and cultural glue holding together the networks of social interaction. Without it, it's hard to imagine how humankind could ever have evolved; but today, we are getting a glimpse of what the world looks like when we fail to think and feel outside of our own bubbles.

Why is empathy becoming rarer?

Perhaps it's generational differences in parenting styles.
Perhaps it's a feature of hyper-individualistic late-stage capitalist societies.
Perhaps the internet has eroded more meaningful forms of human engagement.

Whatever the case (and it's likely to be a mix of all the above and more), you probably picked up this book because you are interested in learning to develop your own capacity to feel for your fellow human being. Whether you have had difficulties in this area in the past or you are someone who wants to improve their natural empathic abilities, you will undoubtedly find something in this book to help.

We'll be looking at what empathy really is and how you can start to be kinder, more understanding, and more compassionate in small ways, today. We'll consider some underappreciated ways to developing an empathic mindset, including how to perspective-switch, what to do to deepen your listening, and how to maintain the orientation of curiosity that is so important for anyone wishing to be more compassionate. Finally, we'll look at ways to take our empathy skills and apply them to trickier situations like conflict, asserting boundaries, or saying no—without jeopardizing a sense of connection.

What Empathy Is

Empathy is a fundamental part our neurobiology (yes, even if you don't currently consider yourself a very empathic person!). Psychologists have elaborated on the idea of **"theory of mind"—the human capacity to understand another person's state of mind and comprehend that they have a mind totally different from our own.** However, this cognitive ability may have evolved from a more primal ability to *feel* someone else's emotional state, i.e., basic empathy.

Way back in the early 90s, researchers at the University of Parma in Italy were studying macaque monkeys (Rizzolatti, 1992). One researcher noticed that when he reached for his food, certain neurons in a macaque monkey's brain activated—as though the monkey himself were reaching for the food. This accidental finding led to the discovery and investigating of "mirror neurons." In 2010, Kuhn et al. found that these neurons are also heavily implicated in the reward circuitry of the brain. This means that when we mirror and sync up with others, it *feels* good. Thus, empathic neural machinery is a big part of what makes communities cooperate—and that's in the animal kingdom, too.

Neuroeconomist Paul Zak has also since identified what he calls the brain's HOME circuit (for human oxytocin-mediated empathy). When someone is in distress, the neurochemical oxytocin is released, encouraging us to engage in nurturing, caring behavior (this hormone is fittingly called the "cuddle hormone" and is released in abundance during sexual activity, breastfeeding, or simple skin-to-skin contact).

All human beings possess these specialized mirror neurons in the brain that have the sole function to coordinate and synchronize social experiences. And all humans possess the hormonal and neurochemical foundation to experience warmth, bonding, and the physiological sensation of compassion.

For example, when you register the sound of someone close to you laughing, it's the mirror neurons that are responsible for preparing your own facial muscles to laugh. If you've ever yawned when someone else yawned, then you'll know just how automatic (and irresistible) this part of our neurological wiring is! When you're upset and you feel as though a hug from your mom literally makes you feel better, that's oxytocin speaking. These perceptive abilities evolved in our species long before we developed our rational ability to cognitively imagine the mind of another person. In fact, even babies have been shown to feel empathy (Uzefovsky et al., 2019).

Empathy, then, is not only theory of mind but theory of heart—and it's hardwired into our brains and bodies.

Though empathy might be in decline today, our neurobiological capacity for empathy is the same as it's ever been. That means that even if you feel like you're out of practice (or never cultivated the skill in the first place), you can always learn to be more empathic.

What Empathy ISN'T

One obvious impediment to being more empathic is wrongly assuming what empathy looks like or requires of us.

We do not necessarily need to have experienced what another person has experienced to have empathy for them. Having had the same experience doesn't predict or guarantee empathy. For example, imagine that someone is waiting for ages in the line to use the lady's restroom, complaining loudly about how inconsiderate people are to take so long and keep everyone waiting. However, the moment they get to the front of the line themselves, they slam the door and proceed to take as long as they like, forgetting all about what they have just experienced. Shared experience does not equal empathy!

Similarly, we do not need to be like someone to have empathy for them. Think about the fact that two siblings of similar age raised in the same household and in the same social context may still fail utterly to understand the other's point of view.

Another empathy myth is that if we experience empathy for another, we are essentially condoning, agreeing with, or acquiescing to their point of view. This is a misconception. Taking on another's point of view is a little like watching a movie. The enjoyment of becoming engrossed in the movie has nothing to do with whether we "agree" with the story or not. We enter into another world and another story, and at the end of it, we get up and leave the movie theater. In other words, feeling into someone else's perspective is a value-neutral act. We are not required to make an appraisal or pass judgment—just observe.

So, we don't need to have shared the experience.

We don't need to be similar to the person having the experience.

And we don't need to have any particular opinion on that experience.

All we need is to *understand the other person's perspective* on that experience through their eyes. That's all. Doing this, we can imagine, for example, that the five-year-old who is afraid of what's under the bed is genuinely terrified, even if we ourselves know there's nothing to be afraid of and don't feel any fear. This means that **empathy is not about any particular *situation* per se, but about a unique individual's *perspective* on it.**

Finally, a note about empathy and being "an empath." While it's undoubtedly true that some people are more naturally empathic than others, this human superpower is not reserved for only a select few. Occasionally, someone with poor boundaries or a confused sense of self will feel overwhelmed by their perception of another person's emotions. This is *not* the same as empathy. If we take the idea of "feeling another's pain" too far, we may actually weaken our ability to show kindness, consideration, and compassion for that person—because we are too engulfed in our own emotions.

As we progress through this book, we'll be keeping a few foundational principles in mind at all times:

- Empathy is a normal human ability that *anybody* can develop—but although it is innate, that doesn't mean it always comes naturally or without effort. We can train our empathy skills just as surely as

we can other human capacities like communication, discipline, or creativity.
- In the same vein, empathy is more about what we **do** than what we **are**. Having empathy is not about good intentions or the right personality traits, but rather about our continued conscious choice to communicate, listen, ask questions, reflect, share, and act with kindness and consideration. This book will show you how.
- Finally, empathy is relational—it's never something we do alone, but with others. It's a collective effort. That's why in the chapters that follow, every principle will be tied back in some way to how we put our newly acquired empathy skills to use in context and in relationships. Some exercises and practices are done alone, but always with the intention of "test driving" them out in the world with a living, breathing human being!

The Three Types of Empathy

Imagine you have gone to visit a well-known and experienced psychiatrist. You tell them about the difficult experiences you're having—seemingly at random, your mind keeps wandering off to frightening and bizarre thoughts. You're horrified by these thoughts. You keep thinking, in particular, of accidentally hurting a small child . . . or perhaps doing it on purpose? It's gotten so bad that when you walked past a baby in a stroller that morning, you couldn't help but imagine snatching it and throwing it into a nearby river. What on earth is wrong with you?

The psychiatrist nods a little, expressionless, and says in a monotone, "Well, that's called *intrusive thoughts*. It's more common than you think. It's probably completely harmless, but we might investigate for OCD if it persists."

Now, this is a doctor who is well respected in their field and knows their stuff. They have given you their professional opinion and may be the only person in your world who has actually studied on an academic level the experiences you're describing. Their appraisal is no doubt helpful.

But it's not exactly comforting, is it?

Later, when you go home, you confide in a close friend about the whole thing, as well as how the psychiatrist appointment was a little underwhelming. The friend immediately gasps and says, "You poor thing! That sounds so scary for you."

The question is, who has done the better job of understanding your perspective? Well, *both* the psychiatrist and your friend are being empathic, but in different ways.

Psychologists Daniel Goleman and Paul Ekman have explained that not all empathy is the same; they've outlined a total of three separate types of empathy.

Cognitive Empathy

This is more akin to perspective-taking (which we will explore in more depth later in the book) or understanding someone's thoughts, mindset, or point of view. Cognitive empathy is empathy based on **knowing** or **understanding** what someone else is going through—it is an intellectual exercise, not unlike what the psychiatrist did when they cross-referenced your story and your list of symptoms against their understanding of certain psychiatric diagnoses.

When we hear about strangers in another country experiencing some misfortune, for another example, we comprehend that they must obviously feel awful. Similarly, we may think, "*I'm* a vegetarian, but cats are meat eaters, so I guess I'll feed Mittens meat." But both these conclusions are reached primarily using our own logic and reason and the knowledge we have about the world (i.e., war is terrible, cats eat meat).

Cognitive empathy is extremely useful because it helps expand our own point of view and gives us a foothold into perspectives other than our own. Without real knowledge and insight into what exactly is going on for another human being, we may never grasp anything else about them, and our connection with them will always be shallow. Cognitive empathy is the foundation on which all other compassion is built.

That said, cognitive empathy on its own is seldom enough, as we see in the above example. Speaking to the psychiatrist, you may have felt *understood*, but a certain warmth and compassion was missing. You might not have felt seen, cared for, or valued in the experience you were having. If you've ever shared a personal problem with someone only to have them blandly offer you a practical solution, you'll have experienced firsthand why cognitive empathy alone is seldom enough!

Emotional Empathy

This is the ability to actually share and take some part in the emotional experience of another person. It's not merely understanding their position from somewhere on the outside, but moving right up close to the feeling and feeling it yourself.

In our example, the friend shows emotional empathy. When you talk to her further, she says, "I've experienced something a little like that before. It's going to sound silly, but when I was a teenager, I was convinced I'd sold my soul to the devil somehow, and I could not put the thought out of my mind. I bet you're feeling really frightened right now. I don't know why this kind of thing happens, but in my case, it did go away eventually. If you don't mind me asking, when did it start?"

You instantly feel like she really *gets* what you're going through. You hadn't considered it before, but when she says the word "frightened," you realize this is exactly how you feel. The psychiatrist told you that intrusive thoughts were common, but your friend seems to really *feel* the truth of this for herself and has reflected it back to you. You feel seen and validated. And you don't feel so alone as you did when sitting in that psychiatrist's office.

Emotional empathy is the stuff that sincere social connections are made of. Emotions—and shared emotions—bind people together. This kind of empathy is the fabric of kindness and compassion, perhaps our very humanity. But again, on its own, it has its limits. Your friend really and truly feels for you—but she has no idea *why* you're experiencing what you are or how to help beyond empathizing.

Another example can show the limits of purely emotional empathy: A father comes home from his insanely stressful and complicated job, feeling exhausted and overwhelmed. His young son has absolutely no idea of the world of anxieties his father inhabits—the bills, the responsibilities, the worries. But he genuinely feels for his father. He doesn't understand the cause of the exhaustion, but with love, he empathizes with it.

Compassionate Empathy

This can also be called empathic concern. It is a position that goes beyond cognitive comprehension of emotion and also beyond the sharing in that emotion. **With compassionate empathy,** *we put our feelings of understanding and sympathy to good use.* **We try to resolve problems, to remove burdens, or to inspire insights that will help progress the situation.**

Even if you had both the psychiatrist and your friend on your side, you'd probably still want some more concrete way out of your predicament. Let's say you then chat with an old family friend who kindly shares what worked for them in a similar situation. Imagine they offer their help directly, asking you what you think you most need right now. Without seeming like a know-it-all or giving unwanted advice, your old family friend suggests a few interesting books you could read or a meditation technique they've personally found useful.

At the end of your conversation with them, you feel that not only have they understood where you're coming from, and not only have they felt along with you, but they've also empowered you to make real changes and improvements. They have shown you compassionate empathy. Not only do they understand and feel your situation, they want to improve it.

So, which form of empathy is "best"? Truthfully, they're best when combined with one another. As you learn to develop your own empathy skills, it might help to imagine that these three types are on a progressing ladder—so start with cognitive empathy, then move to emotional empathy, then finally finish with the most intense form of empathy, which is more active and compassionate.

An example will help. Imagine a friend has just lost their mother to cancer. You send a condolences card. When you next meet, you begin with cognitive empathy and try to understand their thoughts, feelings, and behaviors on a more intellectual level. Maybe you already know that they were on very poor terms with their mother and they hadn't spoken in a decade. Maybe you also know that your friend has never quite forgiven their mother for certain things that happened during childhood.

Putting all this together and using primarily your intellect, you guess that although your friend is probably grieving, they might have lots of other, more complex and difficult feelings surrounding this death, too. Because of this, you don't immediately launch into an overly emotional display where you cry out, "Oh, you must be *devastated*! She was such a wonderful woman!"

As you engage a little with your friend, listening carefully to the answers your questions are receiving, you begin to connect more with them and gradually start to feel what they are feeling. To your surprise, you see that they are actually angry. They say, "I'm really mad at her . . . She just disappeared when there was so much unfinished business. Now what am I supposed to do?" You hear the hurt in your friend's voice and can relate. You, too, have known the pain and confusion of a sudden goodbye and feeling like you never got closure. Your cognitive empathy is morphing into emotional empathy.

After having a heart-to-heart with your friend, you feel comfortable moving to the final, more compassionate form of empathy. You hear them again say, "I just don't know what to do now. I've never planned a funeral." You hear the emotion behind this and decide to step in to help. You liaise with other family members and take some of the funeral admin on yourself, or perhaps you just agree to come over every evening for a while to help tidy up your friend's flat and make sure they have something to eat. Years into the future, this simple act of kindness may be remembered by your friend as the highest form of empathy they received in a difficult time.

You can use the three kinds of empathy in smaller, more everyday ways, too. By ticking all the empathy boxes and gradually progressing to compassionate empathy, we create a feeling of trust.

Try this:
1. Ask about a fact or further explanation to show you want to understand
2. Offer an emotion label or express an emotional response
3. Demonstrate a willingness to help in some way.

Consider the following conversation:

A: "So I flunked the exam. Missed the pass mark by one percent. I'm devastated."
B: "By just one percent? Wow, that really sucks. Is it really not possible to negotiate a pass mark

somehow, being so close?" **(A question geared toward cognitive empathy.)**

A: "Nope. I just chatted with the lecturer, and she's adamant that a fail is a fail. I can't believe it."

B: "Oh man, I'm so sorry to hear that. It must be so ... I don't know, *frustrating* to be so close and yet it's still a flat-out fail." **(A statement coming from emotional empathy.)**

A: "Exactly. It is frustrating. And what's annoying is that I know she's right, and they can't just make exceptions. But now I'm really panicking about the exam next month. I didn't realize I was quite so far behind ..."

B: "Yeah, I get that. I'm sure this has been a knock to your confidence. Hey—if you like, I can come over tomorrow and I'd be happy to help you put together a study plan for the next few weeks. We can go through some past papers together." **(A concrete suggestion for practical help coming from compassionate empathy.)**

A: "Really? That would help, actually. Thanks."

Compassion—A Balancing Act

Renowned shame expert, psychologist, and author Dr. Brene Brown explained in one of her popular TED talks the difference between empathy and sympathy. She explained how sympathy is "feeling for" someone but from a distance and without getting too emotionally connected. It's a little like seeing that someone is trapped in a deep hole, but continuing to stand outside of it, high above them, and talking to them from your position of *not* being in the hole. "Wow, that looks pretty bad. I'm so glad *I'm* not stuck in a hole like that—looks awful!"

A person with sympathy may (annoyingly) try to offer a positive interpretation to the person in the hole, but this doesn't work because it doesn't acknowledge the situation the person is in. If you were in a hole, would you care that a person currently outside the hole can agree that you're in a bind? Would it help for them to say, "Look, it's a beautiful day today . . . at least your hole is not any deeper than it is"?

Sympathy has its limits. Empathy is, to keep the metaphor going, more about feeling *with* someone, i.e., climbing down into the hole to sit next to them. It's accepting a certain level of vulnerability and reaching out to them in a sincere attempt to connect. You are a human being who has also known difficulty, and this allows you to recognize the struggle they're in, even if it's not identical to your own. And as we've seen, compassionate empathy is the person who can climb down into the whole—and bring a ladder with them.

But consider one final possibility: *too much* empathy. This is like getting down into the hole with them and then proceeding to get trapped in exactly the same way as they're trapped. Your empathy may be so great, and you may be so able to feel their pain in your own heart, that you essentially put yourself in exactly the same position. Now there are *two* of you in the hole. Oops! It turns out, a *little* distance from another person's strong emotional reality is not such a bad idea.

As you read through the chapters that follow, try to keep in mind that nobody is expected to be a selfless saint, and that when it comes to empathy, it's all about balance. In empathy, we draw closer to someone's experience. We step out of our own perspective and step into theirs, trying on their set of beliefs, looking through their eyes and feeling with their heart. But we also need to remember that to truly help someone, we need to be at somewhat of a distance from their pain. **It is always a mistake to keep ourselves far removed from the other person's experience—but it's also a mistake to get too tightly engrossed in it.** Neither extreme is likely to be useful to anyone.

On your journey to becoming a more empathic person, try not to forget this constant interplay between *closeness versus distance,* and remember to include all three types of empathy when you engage with others.

Summary

- Empathy is about the ability to take another person's perspective. It is similar to "theory of mind," which is the human capacity to understand another person's state of mind and comprehend that it is totally different from our own. Empathy is not only theory of mind but "theory of heart"—to *feel* other people's emotions—and it's hardwired into our brains and bodies.
- Empathy is not about any particular *situation*, but about a unique individual's *perspective* on that situation.
- Though it is an innate human ability, it is in decline. We need to consciously cultivate and develop empathy.
- There are three kinds of empathy: Cognitive empathy is empathy based on knowing or understanding what someone else is going through, on an intellectual level.
- Emotional empathy is the ability to actually share and take some part in the emotional experience of another person.
- With compassionate empathy, we put our feelings of understanding and sympathy to good use. We try to resolve problems, remove burdens, or inspire insights that will help progress the situation.

- In an empathic interaction, move from cognitive to emotional to compassionate empathy.
- Sympathy is like seeing someone is in a hole, but standing on the outside looking in with concern. Empathy is like getting down into the hole and relating to the person side by side, *with* them.
- Too little empathy is a problem, but so is too much. Becoming overwhelmed in another person's world means we lose perspective—as well as the ability to be of any practical help to them.

Chapter 2: How to Discover and Flex Your Empathy Muscles

Why Reading Makes You More Empathic

"A reader lives a thousand lives before he dies," at least according to George R. R. Martin, American novelist and creator of the fantasy universe that inspired the international TV hit *Game of Thrones*. People read fiction for many reasons, but **one of literature's most unappreciated benefits is that it may actually make you a more empathic human being.**

Reading (or more specifically, reading fiction) can be the perfect tool to help you practice stepping outside of your own perspective and into the perspective of someone else—even if that someone is just make-believe. In the pages of a book, we can go deep inside the hearts and minds of people who inhabit experiences that may be completely alien to our own and see them through our own eyes.

We see what makes the villain tick, and we get to try on the frame of mind that inspires the hero to undertake his feats of bravery. We encounter firsthand the motivations and justifications of people who live in a universe far apart from our own—one that runs on completely different rules.

The great thing is that reading doesn't feel like hard work. Getting inside the heads of the characters is simply something we do to enjoy the story and understand the narrative as it unfolds. The magic is that, somehow, engaging empathically with these narratives makes us better at navigating the perspectives of real people in real life, once we put the book down.

A 2009 paper by Aram and Aviram in the journal *Reading Psychology* suggests that the benefits of reading may be more properly understood as the benefits of *the stories themselves*, since young children tend to show more empathy simply by knowing lots of well-known fairy tales, or having parents who read to them—even if they can't read themselves. Thus, the empathy-power of reading can be gleaned even before someone knows how to read; **the key is in the ability to switch perspectives**.

A 2014 *Journal of Applied Social Psychology* article by Capozza et al. similarly found that teenagers and young adults who read are more empathic and tolerant of differences in others. The decrease in prejudice and bias was credited, in particular, to stories like the *Harry Potter* series, where young readers are encouraged to feel for characters who are treated unfairly or as outcasts, while similarly thinking about their own privileges, blind spots, and unique difficulties.

The authors of the study concluded that reading could make people more tolerant and accepting of immigrants, gay and lesbian people, and refuges, explaining that, "the world of Harry Potter is characterized by strict social hierarchies and resulting prejudices, with obvious parallels with our society." Although the story contains stigma and prejudice of a completely different kind (people with magical powers versus those without), the overall effect is to broaden perspectives and promote understanding.

The very same scientists conducted another piece of research where participants were asked to read the book *Saffron Dreams*. In this fictional story, a Middle Eastern Muslim woman tells of experiencing racism while living in New York. Participants who read the book were tested to have less negative bias against people of different ethnicities or religions when compared to participants who were asked to either read a mere summary of the book or read a non-fiction work.

It's easy to see why reading leads to empathy, and empathy leads to understanding and tolerance. It is far, far easier to accept and understand another if you have stepped inside their point of view.

> *"In spite of everything I still believe that people are really good at heart. I simply can't build up my hopes on a foundation consisting of confusion, misery, and death. I see the world gradually being turned into a wilderness, I hear the ever approaching thunder, which will destroy us too, I can feel the sufferings of millions and yet, if I look up into the heavens, I think that it will all come right, that this cruelty too will end, and that peace and tranquility will return again."*

When we read these words written by Anne Frank in *Diary of a Young Girl*, something special happens. We are no longer reading dry facts about the persecution of those of Jewish heritage during the horrors of the Holocaust. We are no longer standing outside the story, looking in as ourselves, but entering *into* it and experiencing its contours as the characters themselves feel it.

This word "I" is a spell that transports us into the heart and mind of another. The irony is that our empathy only strengthens when we realize how deeply *human* a stranger's experience is, and how similar to our own—i.e., even if we are not Jewish or fourteen years old or hiding in terror from persecution, we nevertheless have felt something of Anne Frank's hope and faith. As our mind runs over the words, "**I** still believe that people are really good at heart . . ." it is as though our brain temporarily believes that it is in fact *we* who have these feelings.

This will explain why research psychologists repeatedly find a link between reading fiction and better scores on empathy tests as well as improved overall social intelligence (Mar et al., 2006; Mar, Oatley & Peterson, 2009, Journal of Personality). Understanding the inner worlds of fictional characters and relating to real people with empathy and perspective is, in other words, *the same activity.*

There is even evidence to suggest that reading fiction makes physiological changes to the brain. In one study, participants were asked to read a historical fiction title, *Pompeii*, about the plight of a man determined to save his wife during the volcanic eruption that decimated the renowned city. Over the period of reading the book, the participants underwent brain scans.

The findings were fascinating: the researchers found increased activity in brain regions associated with sensation and movement—strongly suggesting that just reading about the Pompeii man's plight activated the brain in the same way as if they themselves were having that experience. It would seem that, at least for a few days after reading the story, the participants' brains thought they were inhabiting the body of the main character. Powerful stuff!

So, how can we use this information to deliberately flex our empathy muscles and become better at perspective-taking?

Tip 1: Choose Your Fiction Wisely

You want to **go for literary fiction**—the kind of writing that immerses you in another character's perspective, thoughts, feelings, and world view. All the better if it is written in first person ("I did such and so, and then I felt XYZ"). The classic "bildungsroman" is a novel based around character development and focuses heavily on unique people's psyches and perceptions.

If you're a male professional working in a metropolitan area in central Tokyo, what does it feel like to step into the shoes of a Russian noblewoman living centuries ago, facing the prospect of a doomed marriage during a time of war? If you're a fifty-five-year-old African American mother of three, what does the world look like from the point of view of a sixteen-year-old boy living in rural Scotland, one year after his mother's traumatic death?

Naturally, non-fiction will not have the same empathy-building effect since things like thrillers or crime dramas tend to brush over the inner workings of the characters' lives and focus instead on plot and action. That said, *any* writing that focuses on the inner workings of another person's heart and mind has the potential to stoke the fires of empathy.

Tip 2: Sample Widely

Reading is a superpower. Someone else's story is a vehicle out of your own narrow perception and into something new and outside your own web of understanding and perception. To make full use of this superpower, read a wide variety of different perspectives. You can do this on two levels:

- **Choose authors who are different from yourself**. This means different age, ethnicity, nationality, religion, political affiliation, social class, generation, profession, or culture.
- **Choose books about characters who are very unlike yourself.** Good authors possess the gift of showing you someone else's world from the inside out—and that includes those from other species, time periods, or universes!

You might decide to read on a topic that is personally familiar to you, but derive enormous benefit from seeing it tackled from a wholly different perspective. For example, you may have ancestors that lived through the Holocaust, and you may have read widely on the topic, but what happens when you read an autobiography of some of the German officials who were involved at the time? Perhaps you gain a much richer sense of empathy when you read a firsthand account about life during the time of the Rwandan genocide—an event that is wholly new to you, and yet somehow familiar.

Tip 3: Read ACTIVELY

There is no question that well-written literary fiction can transport you far from the limits of your own perspective. But it can't do the work for you!

Read actively and engage with the story. Consider a particular character and ask yourself:

- How does the current event look from their point of view?
- What do they value, and what are they trying to achieve?
- What is their backstory, and how does it influence their actions right now?
- Ultimately, what is motivating them?
- What are they *not* saying? Consider the things you can infer about them by their

choices, their actions, and what they deliberately choose to conceal or reveal.
- Think about their relationship to other characters in the book.
- If this person were in front of you right now, what kind of a conversation might you have with them?

In one way or another, every story is about the human experience. When you have empathy, you are learning to ask, **"What does the human experience feel like for *this* specific human? Why?"** For example, you may be reading a book about a gay couple in Arizona who are navigating the challenges of adopting a child. If you are not gay yourself, don't want children, and can't imagine going through the adoption process, you could look at their story and think, "This isn't interesting," because to you, the themes are just not relevant.

But the story *does* become relevant when you look at events not from your own point of view, but from theirs. We could ask, **"How would I feel in their shoes?"** but this is not perspective-taking. Empathy, rather, is about asking, **"How do *they* feel in *their* shoes?"** Big difference.

Importantly, you don't have to like or concur with a perspective to take it. Remember that understanding doesn't imply agreement—just understanding. The wonderful thing about perspective-taking is that you can switch right back again! Even if you don't find someone else's world all that interesting, realize that you still gain value simply by exposing yourself to something new. The empathy you cultivate trying to understand the gay couple's point of view may indirectly help foster completely unrelated relationships elsewhere in your life.

Tip 4: Be Discerning

Bearing in mind that literary fiction can literally change your brain, **be cautious about which perspectives you delve into.** The mere fact of changing point of view is a valuable exercise in itself, but not all perspectives are created equally. In an era of fake news, mass-media manipulation, and underhanded political spin in the guise of journalism, it's worth combining literary empathy with intelligent critical thinking.

After all, if you repeatedly read content from a particular person's perspective, there's a good chance it will influence your own over time—or even replace it. Literary fiction is art that is primarily created to explore a theme or aspect of the human condition. But there is a difference between a genuine perspective, an artistic creation, and an artificially constructed point of view designed to influence readers.

As an example, imagine you were reading the book *Saffron Dreams*

"But black reminds me of all that is sad and wrong in my life. Ironically, in this country, it validates my state of being a widow. It is also the color of my hijab—the dividing line between my life with Faizan and the one without him. How different lives are from continent to continent..."

... and discovered that it had not been written by author Shaila Abdullah, but by a twenty-something American male college student who majored in marketing! Changes things, doesn't it? Exploring perspectives is a wonderful thing to do—just be fully aware of whose perspective is being shared, and to what end.

Doctor Sara Konrath, empathy expert and researcher, claims, "I do think that reading books can help to promote more kindness overall. But like any type of media, it probably depends on the content. After all, *Mein Kampf* by Hitler was a book that promoted hate."

Become Emotionally Literate by Labeling

Just as the researchers in the previous chapter discovered that children who read were more empathic, they also discovered that they possessed more sophisticated language skills—which is understandable. There is a close and natural link between comprehending how someone feels and being able to describe that understanding and feeling. In other words, **empathy and "emotional literacy" go hand in hand.**

The emotion wheel helps you develop increased self-awareness, empathic mastery, and precision when it comes to emotions. This may seem at first like a very obvious point, but it's worth noting that to manage, understand, and communicate the complex emotional realities of other people, you need to have a detailed and rich understanding of those emotions . . . a little like an artist needs a fine appreciation of all the countless shades and nuances of color to paint a full and faithful rendition of his subject.

Have you ever heard someone describe themselves as an "intuitive," or claim to be very sensitive or even psychic? They might be. They also might, however, be confusing the *experience* of strong emotions with the *understanding* of those emotions. Having a strong knee-jerk emotional response to an event does not mean you can pinpoint what that feeling actually **is**—or what it isn't. It also doesn't automatically mean you have any self-awareness, compassion, or self-mastery.

If you've ever said something like, "Why did I say that?" or, "I don't even know what I'm feeling right now," then you'll know firsthand that emotional literacy isn't a given. **Emotional literacy is the ability to identify and verbalize complex emotions. It is an act of self-awareness.**

According to the creator of the emotion wheel, Robert Plutchik, there are eight primary human emotions, as well as their more subtle variations. According to Espinoza, a therapist who uses the emotion wheel to teach emotional literacy,

> "Primary emotions are basic emotions that humans are born with that have been wired into our brains. Along the outer edges of the emotion wheel, you'll find low-intensity emotions such as acceptance, distraction, boredom, and so on. As you move toward the center, the color on the emotion wheel deepens and milder emotions become your basic emotions."

Even if you don't quite agree with the basic emotions it lists (and there are variations on this wheel), the basic purpose of such a tool is to gain a systematic understanding of emotions, how they vary in strength, and how they relate to one another. Importantly, the tool is there to help you map specific *words* onto emotional states. After all, it's hard to communicate and engage with another person if you lack a common language to talk about the hidden, inner experiences you're both having.

Astonishingly, Plutchik believed that humans could experience up to thirty-four thousand distinct emotions. However, all of these can be boiled down to the **eight primary ones: sadness, anger, disgust, joy, trust, fear, surprise, and anticipation.** (An even easier heuristic would be to reduce it to four emotions: mad, sad, glad, and fear.)

Sadness, for example, at the center of the wheel and at its most intense is *grief*. At the edges of the wheel, it is less intense and called *pensiveness*. *Disgust* at its most intense is *loathing*; mild disgust is more aptly *boredom*.

Each of these eight also combines with adjacent emotions. For example, the intersection of *surprise* and *fear* creates the emotion of *awe*. Because emotions can be understood as flowing on a spectrum (like color), we can theoretically identify almost infinite shades of emotion, including novel mixes and variations in intensity. Just like color, the emotion wheel also suggests each emotion's "opposite"—for example, *admiration* versus *loathing*, or *ecstasy* versus *grief*.

Too many people assume that having emotions means they're able to understand, label, or communicate emotions—but this is a separate skillset entirely. Sadly, too many people dismiss all emotions into one vague category ("feelings") and believe that the finer nuances are not worth elucidating. Not true! **With greater identification and awareness comes more clarity, insight, and mastery**. And most importantly for our book, it aids empathy—how can you know what another is feeling if you both don't know the word for it?

Our emotions serve a purpose and are there for a reason. We have emotions in the first place because for our ancient ancestors, emotions served a survival purpose and gave those who possessed them a fitness advantage. So, part of gaining emotional literacy is not just learning the names of different emotions, but understanding *why* they emerge, the function they serve, and how they emerge and dissipate in everyday situations.

Sadness

- Originating in the infant human's distress at being separated from a caregiver; a

primal response to loss and abandonment.
- Sorrow, depression, and hopelessness, but also milder versions including lethargy, apathy, and loneliness.
- Contrasting feeling is joy.

Anger

- Genetically programmed response to threat to life or territory, brought about by real or imagined harm or infringement.
- Rage and aggression are the intense versions, whereas milder forms include dissatisfaction or irritation.
- Contrasting feeling is fear.

Disgust

- Biologically rooted response to life-threatening situations, objects, or substances. Designed to get you far away from that which could harm you.
- Loathing and revulsion are on the stronger side, with boredom being a very weak form.
- Contrasting feeling is trust.

Joy

- On a basic biological level, the reinforcing response to life-affirming and successful behaviors.

- Stronger forms include ecstasy and elation, while a weaker form is contentment.
- Contrasting feeling is sadness.

Trust

- An abstract psychosocial experience of safety, and an optimism in the future and the positive behavior of others.
- At its most intense, it is hope and optimism; in its more neutral forms, it may show as curiosity.
- Contrasting emotion is disgust.

Fear

- Perhaps *the* primal emotion; the bodily aversion to danger.
- Its strongest form is terror and panic, while milder forms encompass things like anxiety, uncertainty, or even just frankness.
- Contrasting emotion is anger.

Surprise

- An ancient response that occurs when our expectations and the reality in front of us clash suddenly. This can result in feelings from amusement and disbelief to shock and speechlessness.
- Contrasting emotion is anticipation.

Anticipation

- Feelings of awaiting some assumed future event—first evolved in our species to help us adapt to potential future situations.
- It could take the form of excitement and pleasure, or irritation, uncertainty, and unease.

Reading the above list of eight basic emotions, you might have found them ... well, a little basic. But the magic of the emotion wheel comes in how it's used. Let's consider a few ways to take what is essentially an emotions catalogue and put it to use practically.

Method 1—Identifying Your Own Emotions

Yes, this is a book about empathy, but the truth is that you cannot have heightened awareness of other peoples' emotional states if you are a stranger to your own. In a later chapter, we'll further explore the value of knowing ourselves in order to know others better, but for now, it's enough to say that in any social situation, a mature person owes it to themselves and others to understand what emotions they are feeling, and that these emotions are in fact *theirs* (as opposed to belonging to or stemming from the other person).

Consult the emotion wheel any time you're feeling overwhelmed, confused, or lost. Start at the center of the wheel and tune into your body, seeing which of the basic emotions most fits your physical sensations. How open or closed is your body? Openness suggests anticipation, trust, and joy, while a closed body can signal fear. Is your emotion advancing toward the situation or away from it? The former could suggest a variant of anticipation, the latter of disgust or surprise. How intense is the feeling? Is it changing in intensity over time?

If you're really confused, ask questions to help you decide between two opposites. For example, do you feel more trust or more disgust? You notice your scowling expression—definitely disgust. Are you more afraid or angry? Maybe you notice you want to flee the situation rather than yell or hit something . . . definitely fear, then. After exploring your emotion for a while, you might settle on, for example, a complex feeling of shame and embarrassment, with a tinge of vulnerability.

It may help to consult a comprehensive list of emotions online (there are many available) to help you pinpoint how you're feeling—remembering that emotions are often a mix of several different feelings that can vary in intensity and even in their direction (for example, disgust feels different if it's directed toward another person, an inanimate object, or yourself). If you're stuck, you could work backward and identify what you're definitely sure you don't feel, then consider the emotion on the opposite of the wheel. This may sound pretty obvious until you realize that many of us unconsciously forbid ourselves to experience certain emotions . . . so when we do, we're unable to correctly see the experience for what it is.

It may be helpful to identify the different *components* that make up a larger, more complex emotion. Remember that emotions don't happen in a void—there's always a context, and the emotion is always just one part of a larger, dynamic narrative that's still underway. You may be feeling both joy *and* sadness at the same time, in different proportions. Or you might discover a dynamic pattern where you vacillate between fear and anticipation, first one then the other, each one seeming to cancel the other.

You may even notice something like a main core emotion deep within that is covered superficially by a secondary emotion on the surface. This is because **we can have emotions about emotions**—we may feel *fear*, for example (primary or core emotion), but then feel *anger* at ourselves for feeling that way (secondary emotion). Then when we ask, "How do I feel?" we might answer with "annoyed" or "bored," but this is just the secondary surface emotion. If we dig deep underneath that initial irritation, we will find that we are, in fact, afraid.

If you use the emotion wheel to come to this conclusion, you've given yourself three important benefits:

1. You now have a better, more realistic understanding of what is going on so you can actually do something about it
2. You can give yourself the compassion and understanding you need
3. You can clearly and honestly communicate your experience with others, creating more authentic connections. If there is a conflict, expressing yourself accurately will give you a much better chance of resolving it!

Understanding your own emotions is like making a two-dimensional picture three-dimensional. Emotions give you important contextual information that allows you to engage in intelligent problem-solving, real communication, and self-awareness. In a way, learning to understand your emotions better is taking yourself as your first object for practicing empathy.

Sure, knowing how you feel won't make the emotion magically disappear or solve all your problems, but it's the first small step toward acceptance and self-knowledge. Putting your finger on an overwhelming emotion can be incredibly empowering in the moment because it reminds you that, yes, you are just having an emotion—it is temporary and will pass.

Emotions are not just things that happen to us. We are not simply at their mercy. We can engage with our experience and become curious about it, asking:

What do I feel?

Where is this feeling coming from? Why am I feeling it?

What purpose does this emotion serve?

What happened immediately before I felt like this?

What events, people, situations, or thoughts can I connect this emotion with?

How is my body feeling?

In real life, there will never be an obvious opportunity to sit down and deliberately become aware of your emotions—emotional literacy means consciously choosing to have this awareness. Understanding emotions on an intellectual level is one thing, but the real mastery comes when you can be honest, self-aware, and curious *in the moment while you are experiencing an emotion.* Thus, emotions are easy to understand and easy to master in principle—but not in practice. Let's consider an example.

You get home after spending the day with your parents, and your head is a mess. You crash on the sofa and feel like you've been hit by a bus.

Your partner pokes their head round the corner to ask an innocent question, and you snap at them, causing offense. *Now* is your chance. If you are emotionally intelligent, moments of emotional intensity can be thought of as an invitation to stop, become aware, and gain self-control. You pause and notice where you are—what's going on with you? Why?

You take a few deep breaths and notice how hard this is. You close your eyes and "feel into" this sensation. There's a weird tightness at the back of your throat that feels almost like crying or choking. You become aware that you're frowning and that your fists are balled up. When you deliberately relax your muscles, you notice a flood of emotion coming up in you—it feels awful.

You keep breathing and exploring the sensation with the curiosity of a scientist but the compassion of a good friend. You find the emotion wheel and zoom in on grief and loathing. That feels close to your current experience, but it doesn't make sense—you love your parents and don't want them to fly home tomorrow. What's going on?

After more gentle contemplation and honest inner inquiry, you start to see that this layer of anger is hiding a deeper sense of sadness. Don't you always feel this way when people are saying goodbye? You are happy to see your parents after years of living in different countries, but when you meet, it only seems to drive home the distance between you, and you are simultaneously angry at them and the inevitable goodbye that has to come.

By doing this exercise alone at home, you are in fact completely changing the situation, even if it doesn't seem like it initially. You are less likely to be irritable with your partner and more likely to share your real feelings with your parents at the airport the next day, rather than make a snarky comment about never seeing them again. What's more, you are able to better process your sadness—and move on from it.

According to Espinoza, identifying emotions is the first step to moving through and past them: "It is imperative to name our emotions and know what we are feeling in order to **prevent an intensification of emotions**, which can result when we don't deal with or confront our emotions. The emotion wheel is a helpful tool that helps one identify their feelings and become comfortable in sitting and feeling their emotions."

Method 2—Identifying the Emotions of Others

Compassion, awareness, acceptance, curiosity— the great thing about all these qualities is that when we develop them in ourselves, we simultaneously develop our ability to feel them for others. The more perceptive we are about our own emotional states, the better we are able to appreciate other people's. We can use our own emotional experiences as a kind of bootstrap; no, we will never know exactly what it feels like to be another person, but we know what it feels like to be us. Because all humans share the same basic physiological emotions, our feelings and experiences can be a bridge or a shared language into the emotional experiences of another person. We can access another person's world via their rational, cognitive mind, and by examining their thoughts and perspectives—but this is always going to be superficial when compared with the real flesh-and-blood lived experience of emotion.

The first (counterintuitive) step to being more empathic is to become more emotionally literate within yourself. This finetunes your focus, your awareness, your emotional vocabulary, your ability to accept with open curiosity, and—this is a big one—take responsibility for your own feelings so you don't project them onto others. You can take this emotional mastery into every interaction with others.

The process to being aware of *another person's* emotions is not dissimilar from the process described above:

1. Pause and become aware without judgment or avoidance

2. Notice first the reaction and response of the *body*
3. Identify a primary emotion on the emotion wheel
4. Keep asking questions or making observations to home in on more subtle variations of the primary emotion

Imagine, for example, that your parents have come to visit and you are out having a drink with your father. You pause and deliberately ask yourself, "What is he feeling? What is his emotional reality right now?" You listen carefully and watch his behavior with compassionate curiosity. You see that despite laughing and making small talk with the bar staff, his body seems tight and stiff, and he is avoiding eye contact.

You think about the emotion wheel and try to imagine which core emotion matches up with this physical experience of rigidity and "closedness." Taking into account other contextual clues and what you already know about your father, you begin to see that he is in fact quite anxious—a moderate expression of the primary emotion of fear. You notice also that it started when you entered the bar. In fact, as you observe the raised shoulders and tightened jaw muscles, you realize that you yourself also feel a little on edge—perhaps in sympathy with him.

The bill comes and your father makes a rude comment about the price of the drinks, and it all falls into place—he is anxious about spending too much money. You smile and offer to pay the bill and suggest that you leave and find something more relaxed (and free!) to do next. "I can see you're a little on edge. What do you say we get out of here?"

In that moment, your father may well feel like you've read his mind. But you've merely shown a little empathy. Had you *not* had this empathy, you would have looked at his smiling face and assumed all was well—and he would have grown more and more irritable and anxious with every new drink that was ordered. Instead, by recognizing his emotion, you were able to navigate this simple social situation in a way that created more understanding, harmony, and connection.

This brings us to a final consideration when it comes to the emotions of others: We don't always have to guess! Depending on the relationship with your father, you might have been able to say, "Hey, it seems like you're a little anxious right now. How are you doing?" When we tentatively volunteer a label for the emotion another person might be feeling, we are doing three things:

1. Helping them gain more self-awareness of their own emotions
2. Confirming our observation and giving them a chance to help us adjust our understanding ("No, not anxious exactly, but I am a bit annoyed at spending so much on a cocktail...")
3. Demonstrate to the other person that we are present, that we are listening, and that we care about witnessing their emotional state and getting its name right

Cautiously suggesting an emotion label for someone else's experience is a great way to signal that you want to be empathic... which is a big part of being empathic! It opens a dialogue. It creates more intimacy and connection. Even if you don't "guess" correctly, you are inviting the other person to share a little of themselves. If you *do* guess correctly, you may create a precious moment of understanding and trust—the stuff that relationships are made of!

The trick is to be subtle and gentle rather than trying to forcefully label someone or interpret their experience within your own framework. Make a suggestion, then pull back and listen, noting the response.

"You seem a little _____ right now."

"Wow. Do you think you felt _____ when that happened?"
"Would you say you're feeling kind of _____ about it?"

Start with a core emotion and let the other person do the finetuning.

A: "Oh, that sounds so **sad**."
B: "Well, yes. Sad but also really **disappointing** at the same time, you know?"
A: "I get it. It seems like you're really **disheartened** by the whole thing..."

If you're really at a loss, just use the same words or imagery the other person is using, or look for a close synonym. If they have said the word "stressed" to you five times in the last two minutes, then reflect this back to them by saying something like, "This must be such an anxious time for you!" Play it by ear but keep it light—just remember that nothing is more infuriating than an amateur psychologist putting words in your mouth instead of listening to what you're actually telling them!

Summary

- Reading literature may actually make you a more empathic human being. It can reduce bias and prejudice and literally change your

brain physiology. The key is in the ability to switch perspectives.
- Choose literary fiction, preferably written in first person. Try authors who are different from yourself, or books about characters that are unlike yourself.
- Read actively and engage with the story. Pause to ask questions to investigate the character's point of view, switching perspectives and exploring motivations and desires. Ask yourself, "What does the human experience feel like for *this* specific human? Why?" Instead of asking how you would feel in their shoes, ask how *they* feel in their shoes. However, be discerning about what kind of perspectives you delve into!
- Another way to build empathy is to create "emotional literacy." Emotional literacy is the ability to identify and verbalize complex emotions. It is an act of self-awareness. With greater emotional identification and awareness comes more clarity, insight, and mastery—and better empathy.
- The emotion wheel is a helpful tool that helps you develop increased self-awareness, empathic mastery, and precision when it comes to emotions. It outlines shades and nuances of the eight primary emotions: sadness, anger, disgust, joy, trust, fear, surprise, and anticipation.

- We can use the emotion wheel both to identify and explore our own emotions and to identify and empathize with the emotions of others. To empathize with others' emotions, pause to become aware, notice their body language, then identify a primary emotion on the emotion wheel. Keep asking questions, making observations, or offering emotion labels to home in on exactly what they're feeling.

Chapter 3: Accounting for Bias, Prejudice, Ego, and Perspective

Root Out Bias and Prejudice

Emotional literacy and awareness of your own emotions are two great ways to become a more empathic person.

But, even with emotional intelligence and self-awareness, you can still fail to have real empathy if you hold on to bias and prejudice. **A pre-conceived notion about who another person is may be the single biggest obstacle on the path to genuine empathy for them.** Prejudice and bias are two major blind spots; to be more empathic, we need to take responsibility for them and commit to being more open-minded.

When people hear the words "prejudice and bias," they may immediately think of things like racism or sexism, or jumping to conclusions about those with disabilities or people from a religion they don't really understand. Can things like racism and sexism get in the way of genuine empathy? Of course. But the question of prejudice and empathy goes much, much deeper than this.

Let's pause for a moment and look a little more closely at an interesting word: "kin." You'll see traces of it in English words such as *akin* (meaning "alike" or "similar in kind"), kinship, and kindred. This word has Indo-European roots and come from the old Germanic term meaning "to give birth to." This root also branches from the old Norse term *kundr* (meaning child). Your kin, then, are those who are your family. The related Old Saxon term *kunni* refers to "kind, race, or tribe," the Dutch *kunne* means "sex or gender," and the Old English *cynn* means "family, race, kind, sort, rank, or nature." So, we can understand the word to refer not just to blood family, but to tribes, community, and those who are similar to us.

But we can also see traces of this interesting word's history in the two meanings of "kind"—a word used to depict compassion and kindness, as well as type, class, or family—"he lived with his kind." The implication is that if someone is of your kind, you are kind to them.

Without going much deeper into the etymology, it should be clear that for human beings, there are powerful and ancient connections between sameness and compassion. It is a given that we are empathic toward our own kind and less so to those who are strange and unknown to us. Again, we see that for human beings, our emotional reality has a deep and ancient physiological basis—after all, isn't maternal love the prototype for all other forms of human kindness? Don't we speak of "brotherly love" as the highest and strongest bond between human beings?

To return to bias and prejudice, then: whenever we pre-judge (the root of the word "prejudice"!), we decide that a person is unlike ourselves. They're not in our family or tribe. And when we do that, we deliberately close off a potential feeling of kinship and connection with them. While it is true that human beings belong to many different groups that are genuinely not alike, the mere fact of classing another human being into a category different from our own makes it harder to feel that they are our "kin"—in other words, to have empathy for them.

So, what does it really mean to remove bias and prejudice in yourself? It does not mean that we "live and let live" but rather that we make the choice to recognize the *similarity* between ourselves and others. In other words, empathy can only thrive when we remove barriers of difference and focus instead on affiliation. It is not true empathy to simply say, "Well, you do you," or, "I guess you have the right to your opinion!" and shrug your shoulders. It is not true empathy to cling to differences and begrudgingly "tolerate" them.

Here's a question: What is the single thing that unites every human being you will ever encounter? Across gender, race, class, income level, religion, culture, age . . .? The only thing that makes us *all* part of the same family is the fact that we are **human beings.** When we have bias and prejudice, we encounter a person primarily as a class or category, forgetting that we both belong to the bigger category: human beings.

So, we encounter someone and experience them not as a human being, but as a woman, or a Mormon, or a five-year-old, or a prisoner, or a cancer survivor, or a widow, or an Australian. We have our own preconceptions about what each of those categories means, so when we engage with that person, we are not actually engaging with the human being that they are, but instead with the stereotype that belongs to that category. Women are nurturing, prisoners are bad people, Australians all love surfing.

These categories may be a handy mental shortcut when dealing with the complexity of humankind, but at the same time, the stereotypes they create distance and *undermine authentic connection with the real human being in front of you.* Through these stereotyped filters, all the information we receive about that person is distorted.

For example, if a person sees a tiny infant wearing blue who is screaming, they may say, "Poor baby! Look how angry he is!" This response is colored by their assumptions and prejudices about gender. That same person may see the same baby screaming, but if the baby is wearing pink, they may instead say, "Poor baby! Look how scared she is!" In both cases, there is empathy, but it is distorted. **What distorts it? Prejudice. Pre-judging what another's experience is and what it means.**

Of course, it would be foolish to expect anyone to operate in the world without *some* preconceived ideas about stable and persistent patterns of human behavior (for example, on the whole, women really *are* more nurturing than men). At the same time, wildly inaccurate biases and prejudices can be a serious roadblock to understanding another person's unique, complex, and subtle inner world. In a way, prejudice is the very opposite of empathy.

In empathy, we can engage with another person in the spirit of, "Who are you? What is it like to be you?"

In prejudice and bias, we are not curious and we are not asking a question. Instead, we engage with another in the spirit of, "I already know who you are, and I know just what you're like."

Importantly, being empathic is not just about being kind. It's about clear, accurate perception and genuine comprehension of another worldview. After all, many people are genuinely compassionate and want to be kind to others, but their fixed ideas of what that should look like still get in the way of genuine connection. Think about the example of a mother who keeps trying to "treat" her daughter by giving her spa days and beauty products as gifts.

The mother has preconceived ideas about what daughters are like and what they think, feel, and want. Because of her prejudice, she cannot see that from her daughter's perspective, these things are not treats at all. The mother is kind without being empathic. Sadly, without empathy, she is missing out on an opportunity to be more deeply and authentically kind.

How to Tackle Your Own Biases and Prejudice

Yes, you do have them! Everybody does.

The difficult thing is that our most stubborn and unchallenged prejudices are the ones most likely to go unnoticed. You see an unassuming overweight old woman at the bus stop and have an automatic assumption about who she is. You never give her a second thought—but had you struck up a conversation with her, you would have realized that she is a legendary Hungarian concert pianist and can speak five languages.

A 2005 article in *New Scientist* explored the fascinating research taking MRI images of participants' brains as they responded to images of different people. The results showed that we all have unique brain responses to exposure to different people—in this case, there were definite differences in how people responded to African American faces. The thing is, these brain responses are automatic, immediate, and unconscious—meaning we don't even realize that we have made these snap decisions.

Similarly, Harvard University's now-famous "Implicit Association Test" is designed to reveal these knee-jerk unconscious responses and find out your true beliefs and perceptions. If you Google implicit.harvard.edu, you can take the test yourself—but be prepared to be surprised by the results!

The good news is that we acquired these prejudices and biases by the way we were brought up, by our cultural training, by exposure to the media, by the way we were educated, and in many cases, by our own personal history. This is good news because it means that prejudice is not a fact of life—we can change it.

Step 1: Acknowledge that You DO Have Bias

This goes beyond racism, sexism, and the like—you may have a whole host of prejudices about even seemingly small ways that people can differ. Think about your beliefs about those who didn't go to college, those who listen to the kind of music you hate, those who grew up abroad . . . sometimes, we can be even *more* biased against people who are objectively most like us. For example, someone may feel an irrational hostility toward someone with the same but differently spelled name, or look down on those who speak their language but with a slightly different regional accent. Point is, it doesn't have to be full-blown bigotry to count as prejudice!

Step 2: Expose Yourself to Difference

If your goal is to be a more empathic person, you need to **accept the challenge of having to empathize with *difference* and not just with similarity.** If you want to connect with people, you need to connect with them as they are, in all their strange and unfamiliar uniqueness!

Often, we decide who is in our group and who is out of it simply by habit and convention. We learn to assume that what we already know is good, and that what is unknown must be weird, bad, or threatening. But the best way to prove to yourself that this isn't true is to keep on exposing yourself to difference. For example:

- If you always find yourself feeling hostile to and uncomfortable around homeless people, challenge yourself to volunteer for a few nights at a homeless shelter.
- If you notice that you have negative prejudice toward the opposite sex, consciously choose to read books, blogs, and articles by men/women, especially ones written from *their* unique point of view.
- If you suspect you've placed yourself in a bit of an echo chamber perspective-wise, deliberately seek out the opinions of those you disagree with. Do this in good faith and seek out the most intelligent arguments against your pet theories and beliefs.

- Try food, music, literature, and art from other cultures—bonus points if you can find material that shows you what *you* look like through the eyes of some other group!

Step 3: Connect and Find Common Ground

Our primitive monkey minds evolved to zoom in on potentially life-threatening differences in others. Counter this tendency by choosing instead to **focus on what is common instead**. When you meet a new employee at work, and she's a dark-skinned woman wearing a colored head scarf, don't immediately narrow in on these facts—instead, focus on the fact that she is, for example, the same age as you and, evidently, in the same line of work.

Even the most wildly different person you meet *will always* have something in common with you: They're a human being. They feel all the same emotions as you do. At the very least, you can often connect with people over the very fact of your difference. Expat communities, for example, can often find commonality in the fact that they are all different from the locals. The fact they are different from one another is less important! Similarly, someone who is discriminated against because of their race may find a willing friend in someone who is discriminated against because of their religion—again, we see that the shared experience of human emotion shows us how alike we are, despite and even because of our differences.

The next time you meet someone who feels "other" to you, ask yourself to try to see what connects you both. Everyone loves cute animals, their families, and good food. Nobody likes advertising, horrible weather, or traffic. The commonality you find is unimportant; what matters is the state of empathy you create when you assume that there *is* something in common . . . you just haven't discovered it yet.

Compassion—on the Other Person's Terms

Everyone can agree that it's a good thing to drop prejudice and bias—theoretically. But it's important to realize that empathy is something we **do**, not an opinion we have or a nice intention we hold passively. Furthermore, **the very meaning of compassion, kindness, and empathy changes depending on the recipient**. Consider the following example.

Jamie thinks of himself as a likeable guy, an extrovert, and pretty switched on in the emotional intelligence department. However, he has trouble realizing that his *desire* to think of himself as a fair and good person is not quite the same as doing the hard work of being empathic in real life. Jamie has a new friend, Ed, who is on the autism spectrum. The two have a shared hobby and met at work.

One day, during after-work drinks with a group of colleagues, Jamie notices that Ed is sitting pretty quietly, unsmiling. Because he wants to be kind and compassionate (and also because, unconsciously, he wants to prove to everyone that he has no biases against those with disabilities!), he rushes to Ed's aid. He tries to "cheer him up" and rope him into the conversation. He draws attention to Ed, remarking about how quiet he's being and making obvious attempts to "bring him out of his shell" with jokes, questions, and pointed comments. He feels that, as the group's extrovert, it would be kind to help Ed feel included.

However, after an hour of this dynamic playing out, Ed gets visibly upset and leaves, much to Jamie's confusion.

Another colleague at the table says, "Jamie, you can't be like that. You've got to just accept Ed for who he is."

Jamie is hurt and perplexed. "But that's exactly what I'm doing! Trying to include him. He was just sitting there all by himself."

"Exactly. *That's how he is.*"

Can you see what happened and why? Jamie *was* showing compassion—but compassion on his own terms. He treated Ed the way he—Jamie—would like to be treated. But the so-called Golden Rule ignores the fact that we are all different and want different things. Jamie was unable to have real empathy and see things from his friend's point of view. If he had done so, he might have seen that for Ed, being left to socialize to the degree he felt comfortable was precisely how he would most feel included in the group.

Sometimes, our very attachment to the idea of ourselves as empathic, kind, and warmhearted is precisely the thing that gets in the way of us seeing what other people actually want. Call it a positive prejudice! When we practice empathy, we go into another person's world—all the way in! **We don't just look at them through the lens of our own values and systems of meaning. We look at them as they look at themselves** according to *their* worldview. From Jamie's perspective, being a little aloof and quiet is a big problem requiring intervention. But from Ed's point of view, it's a comfortable default.

When you practice empathy with the people around you, be mindful of the fact that empathy is not for or about *you*—it's for and about the other person. You are not just curious about the contents of their heart and mind, but the very way they construct their reality. To make the mindset shift to genuine empathy, **stop asking the question, "How do I see this person?" and start asking, "How does this person see themselves?"** No matter who you're with, you will instantly dissolve any pre-existing biases, assumptions, and prejudices, and simply see the unique person in front of you. On their own terms.

The Fine Art of Perspective-Taking

To take on another's perspective is to have empathy with them, plain and simple.

Let's look at the story of the woman who has been called "The Mother of Empathy"—Patricia Moore. During 1979 to 1982, she went "undercover" and experienced life as an elderly woman. With professional makeup, wigs, and prosthetics, she gave everyone the impression of being far older than she was.

But she went a step further and wore glasses that clouded her vision, earplugs that made her slightly deaf, and a series of braces, splints, and bandages that impaired her movement. She didn't just want to imagine what it felt like to be old—she wanted to feel it firsthand. In fact, the insights she gained during her experiments led to the creation of easy-open cereal packs and specially designed kitchen implements, i.e., "empathic design."

In a similar way, George Orwell, famed *1984* author, went undercover in 1927 to experience homelessness firsthand, and his experiences changed him forever. Countless mental health reforms have been inspired by those who went undercover in the insane asylums of the past, such as Nellie Bly, who had herself committed into *The Women's Lunatic Asylum* on Blackwell's Island. According to her, "It is only after one is in trouble that one realizes how little sympathy and kindness there are in the world." A perfect summary of the kind of empathy that is possible when we fully inhabit the perspective of another!

In a previous section, we cultivated empathy for another using three different lenses of our own, leading to cognitive, emotional, or compassionate empathy. But we can turn this around and consider the same process from another person's perspective. Perspective-taking is a whole set of skills that includes:

- Understanding someone's **perceptual** assessment of reality
- Understanding someone's **cognitive** appraisal of reality
- Understanding someone's **affective** or emotional response to that reality

The "lens" through which any of us see the world is made of different components. When we wish to take on another person's perspective, we need to consider their position on *all* these multiple levels (what's more, we need to consider how our perspective influences our ability to see their perspective!).

Imagine the following scenario. An old school friend comes to visit you in your new city to meet your new spouse and catch up after more than a decade of not being in touch. You mention more than once in passing how glad you are to have moved to where you now live, how happy you are there, and how much nicer life is. One night, while everyone is enjoying a drink together in your new home, you raise your glass and give a toast, saying, "Here's to leveling up . . . and getting the hell out of (your old hometown)!" Everyone laughs and toasts, but then your old school friend says bitterly, "Hear, hear, and do us all a favor and don't come back," before slamming down their glass and stomping out.

What's happened here? You were having a nice time with friends, in a celebratory mood, and expressing pride and gratitude for all the good things life has sent your way. But a little empathy would show you that this is *not* what your old school friend saw. You take the time to set aside your own experience and go into theirs instead. Instead of stubbornly sticking to your own appraisal of events ("What's *his* problem, anyway?"), you switch perspectives and go into his.

And the moment you do, you realize that it is in fact you who has been unreasonable. Your friend came to visit you at great expense—in fact, they've barely ever left your hometown at all since it's not financially viable for them. They've stayed in the same neighborhood you both grew up in—the neighborhood that you now so readily denigrate.

Perceptual perspective: They see that you have more money, are happier, and are feeling confident in your new life. They see others praising and admiring you. Though you may feel that you worked hard for your success, they may see something different—that you are a little judgmental about where you came from and are now superior to the good people you grew up with. They also see that you seem to be unable or unwilling to acknowledge the obvious difference in your lives and the awkward position the visit puts them in.

Cognitive perspective: They may have many thoughts about this dynamic. "He thinks he's better than me." "He invited me over here so he can rub it all in my face and show off."

Affective perspective: Beneath all this, understandably, is shame, embarrassment, resentment, and all the feelings you'd expect if you believed that someone judged you unfairly. Even further beneath that, you can imagine a genuine feeling of sadness—weren't you once really close friends? In trashing your hometown, are you also saying that your friendship was worthless, too . . . ?

Put all together, this perspective more than explains your friend's reaction. When you pause and literally try to imagine what it must be like for him from his point of view, not only does his behavior suddenly make more sense, but you instantly get a sense of how to make peace again and how to smooth over the conflict. That's because you get an inkling of what *you* look like to him.

You talk to him, you listen, you apologize, and you try to understand his perspective without forcing your own ("You're taking things personally. I never meant any offense!"). Gradually, bridges are mended and hurt feelings forgotten.

As you can see, empathy is not just useful for supporting someone in difficulty—it's also the only real way to dissolve tensions, settle grudges and misunderstandings, and find mutually satisfying solutions to tricky problems. In this case, it also comes to our aid when we have been thoughtless ourselves and need a little empathy to put things right.

Two Essential Ingredients for Walking in Another's Shoes

Ingredient 1: Know exactly what YOU'RE bringing to the table.

To thoroughly comprehend another person's perspective, you need to take responsibility for your own. To remove your own assumptions, biases, and interpretations from the big picture, you need to know what they are in the first place!

More than this, though, it's worth understanding the *why* of how you arrived at your particular perspective (and this includes the perceptive, cognitive, and affective components, as described above). The more comfortable you are with understanding the mechanics of your own position, the better able you'll be to understand those of another.

For example, if you grew up in a major city and your upbringing contained plenty of people, bustle, and culture but very little in the way of plant or animal life, you may discover that this background influences your opinion on pet ownership, on what counts as tidy, and on the ethics of factory farming. Because you can grasp these links, you are all the more able to see how someone who grew up on a farm may have markedly different opinions on all three of those topics.

In the above example, you may discover that you have a particular cognitive perspective that goes like this: "If I didn't *intend* to harm anyone, then I shouldn't be held responsible for any harm that happens." Only by being aware that you think this way can you consciously set it aside so you don't get defensive and think that your friend is blaming or attacking you when you were unaware of the hurt you caused.

Every time you are engaging with someone, ask what assumptions and beliefs you're bringing to the encounter. Where did they come from? How was that process different for the person in front of you? How are the two interacting?

Ingredient 2: Learn to take a back seat and let others lead.

One of the biggest ways people tend to allow their own perspectives to dominate interactions is in their desire to lead. We can sometimes derail or dominate when we want to steer the conversation toward ourselves or the topic we're most comfortable with.

But that's not all. If you're a very literal and practically minded person who views everything through the lens of the scientific method, for example, you might be tempted to always shape and influence conversations in that direction. If the person in front of you is trying to be lighthearted and a little irreverent, your constant desire to be precise, rational, and serious is going to be felt as a misunderstanding and deeply un-empathic.

Empathy is not just a question of allowing others to lead in terms of conversational *content*. It's also about allowing them to determine the style, tone, and pace of conversation. Think of it in terms of movie genres—some people want a romantic comedy; others want a gritty war documentary. The very same events can be told in either genre. If you are truly empathic, you're not just listening to and reflecting the *what*, but the *how*. The other person takes the lead, and you follow happily.

Perspective-Taking, Step by Step

Let's slow down the whole process of perspective-taking and look at each step in detail.

Step 1: Notice the social situation you're in and the people around you.

Step 2: Become aware of the fact that you are thinking about them, and they are thinking about you.

Step 3: Think about why the other people are in this particular social situation; what they might be perceiving, thinking, and feeling; and what their potential motivations or overall intentions might be. How are they behaving? How and why are they behaving this way?

Step 4: Become aware of the fact that these other people may be having the same thoughts about you. They may also be trying to understand your thoughts, feelings, and motivations in this social situation.

Step 5: If necessary, adjust what you are doing or saying to influence the way that other people may be thinking and feeling about you. At the same time, be aware that other people may be doing precisely the same thing. Realize that you are both doing this in line with your perceptions and motivations.

The above five steps can be visualized as a grid or matrix, containing everything that an empathic person can become aware of:

- What the other person thinks about themselves
- What the other person thinks about you
- What you think about them
- What you think about yourself

Let's take a look at an example and how using this grid or the five steps can help you gain a more multidimensional understanding of a social situation. Imagine you are tasked with interviewing a new employee for your division. This is not your usual role, and you've never interviewed anyone before—to be frank, you're a bit nervous. However, a little empathy (before, during, and after the interview) can put everyone's anxieties at ease and make the entire interaction flow a little more smoothly.

- **What the candidate thinks about themselves** – Putting yourself in their shoes, you predict they'll be nervous and hyper-alert (who wouldn't?) and may potentially be feeling somewhat uncertain about themselves. When you meet, you see that the candidate actually seems to be downplaying their resume highlights.
- **What the candidate thinks about you** – Beforehand, you try to imagine what people generally think of their interviewers: that they're cold and judgmental, or perhaps that they're extremely knowledgeable and have high standards. The candidate likely thinks they have to impress you, and they don't know how many other people you've interviewed for this position. You also realize that this candidate actually has no idea that you haven't interviewed anyone before, and has not even considered the fact that you also find the process anxiety-provoking!
- **What you think about the candidate** – When you meet, you find them likeable and well-qualified, if a little unconfident. But you weigh up these perceptions with

everything else you know about the situation.
- **What you think about yourself** – You realize that you're nervous and worried about doing a good job, but on reflection, this allows you to empathize with the candidate, who is probably having similar feelings. Though nervous, you do have faith that you can conduct the interview properly.

In this situation, your main goal is to get the best possible idea of the candidate's suitability for the job. Their goal is to put their best foot forward and convince you to pick them.

Using empathy to take various perspectives on the situation, you decide on a course of action: You deliberately work to come across as friendly, non-judgmental, and casual. You openly admit that this is not your usual role and that you've never interviewed people before. You do this to put yourself at ease, but also to address fears from the candidate's perspective. If they can relax in your company and see that you're not really a stern and serious judge, they may be able to more confidently share their achievements.

In this example, empathy radiates throughout the social situation—by switching perspectives, you bring compassion and understanding to the entire interaction, showing empathy to *both* yourself and the other person.

Perspective-taking is also a rock-solid way of smoothing over conflict or disagreement. If you're mulling over a point of contention, take a moment to analyze the situation in private, fleshing out as many perspectives as you can. Ask yourself:

What are your goals here and what are the other person's? Are they in alignment or clashing?

What assumptions might you be making? What about them?

How have each of you behaved, and can you find out the root cause of each choice?

How does the conflict look from their perspective? How do you think they are discerning the situation as seen through their own perceptual filters?

What exactly is bothering you most about the conflict? How does it compare to their position?

Perspective-taking usually allows one of two things to happen: either the additional empathy helps you appreciate their perspective and the conflict dissolves, or you realize that with too many assumptions and unknowns, the only way forward is sincere communication so that everyone is on the same page. If we're honest, most of the time, our conflicts arise when we have not even communicated, let alone *mis*communicated! The conflict lies, in other words, purely in the fact that each party does not understand the perspective of the other.

Your perspective is a thing of wonder—it is what makes you unique and what brings color, depth, and meaning to your world. However, it's also a potential source of isolation, conflict, and misunderstanding if you forget that it is only that—a perspective—and that other people are in possession of points of view that are just as unique, colorful, deep, and meaningful as your own.

Before we conclude our chapter, here are a few practical exercises to fine-tune the skill of perspective-taking.

- Try a creative writing exercise where you sit down and write, but from the other person's perspective. Use "I" statements and explore their perceptions, thoughts, feelings, intentions, fears, and indeed how they perceive you and the situation at large. This can be a seriously eye-opening practice.
- Watch a movie or TV show and pick a character to identify with. As you watch, try to imagine what they are thinking and feeling. Try to understand why they behave as they do, and what the bigger story feels

like from their frame of reference. Can you predict what they might do or say next, given their perspective? You could watch the same episode again but focus on another character—how does that change things?

- Search online or in magazines for random pictures of people in different situations. Take turns to inhabit the perspective of each person in the picture. Create a story behind the picture and explore each person's perspective on that story.
- Alternatively, indulge in a bit of "people watching" in a public place and do the same by observing groups of people in social situations. As though you were switching camera lenses, try on the situation from different people's points of view. You could also just pick a person in a crowd and ask yourself broadly, "What's it like to be such a person?"
- Try "reverse storytelling." This is when you observe someone's behavior/reaction/words and try to think of potential reasons that could have caused that outcome. As you identify causes, keep going further back to identify causes for those causes, and so on.

Summary

- Your perspective on life is what makes you unique, but it can also be a source of isolation, misunderstanding, and conflict.

- A pre-conceived notion about who another person is may be the single biggest obstacle on the path to genuine empathy for them. Getting rid of bias is about more than guarding against sexism or racism and more about consciously choosing to remember that all people are united in their shared humanity.
- Prejudice is pre-judging what another's experience is and what it means. Stereotypes and categories undermine authentic connections with others. Bias is a filter through which all the information we receive about that person is distorted. Being empathic is not just about being kind. It's about clear, accurate perception and genuine comprehension of another worldview.
- To tackle your own prejudice, first acknowledge that you do have it! Consciously choose to expose yourself to the unfamiliar and challenge yourself to empathize not just with similarity but with difference. Assume there is always a common ground between you and another individual and actively choose to focus on that instead of what is different.
- Forget the Golden Rule and remember that the very meaning of compassion, kindness, and empathy changes depending on the recipient. Show people compassion, but on *their* terms, not yours.

- In interactions, try to explore: what the other person thinks about themselves, what the other person thinks about you, what you think about them, and what you think about yourself. This can be especially helpful during a conflict.

Chapter 4: Listening is Empathy in Action

Don't Just Listen Actively, Listen Empathically

In this chapter, we're going to elaborate on the principle of **getting our own egos and preconceptions out of the way** so we can more clearly and genuinely see the person in front of us—i.e., empathize. When we listen to another person, we are not just being quiet and giving them a turn on the soapbox. Rather, we are creating an open space for them to *be themselves*. Their real selves.

To inhabit another person's worldview and deeply comprehend their state of mind and heart, you first need to actually know what it is. And this means listening. Too often we listen with an agenda. We hear the person, but as we listen, we are busy:

- Deciding whether we agree or not

- Deciding how much their situation or opinion is like ours
- Thinking of something we can say that is similar to what they're saying . . . but which is about us
- Thinking about whether their account is accurate and reasonable, or whether we trust their recollection or the conclusions they're coming to
- Making a judgment on the rationality or appropriateness of their experience
- Trying to find an overarching theme of theory to put their experience in a neat little box
- Dreaming up solutions to their problem, including the problem of how they feel
- Listening for only those things we already know, like, or understand, and ignoring the other bits
- Thinking of the interesting and impressive thing we will say once they stop talking...

And so on. The temptation to do all the above is strong. But when we listen, that's all we do. Listen. Nothing else. Temporarily, we immerse in the world of another and step out of our own. In this new world, the other person is telling the story, and they decide what things mean. Our only job is to witness it as it's told. To do this, we suspend our own ego, our own assumptions—

i.e., our own story—so that we can more clearly comprehend theirs.

Empathic listening, then, is hard work! **It requires us to be sensitive, alert, and respectful.** We need to make an emotional connection. We need to open our perception so that we are genuinely hearing without judgment or without putting our own interpretations and assumptions into the mix. Empathy requires that we are accepting, supportive, and encouraging, yes. But our FIRST job is just to be completely one hundred percent present.

Empathic listening is not just passively keeping quiet, but rather a subtle art composed of many separate skills.

Skill 1: Maximum Attention

You've probably noticed—people all over the planet are seriously unhappy. Many people feel depressed, sad, lost, and alone. In an age of fractured attention spans and the relentless pressure to market and promote oneself as a product, many of us are feeling ignored, unseen, and unknown. The world around us is morphing and re-shaping in complex and sometimes threatening ways, and yet one thing remains the same: Human beings all have a deep, almost primal hunger to belong. We all want to feel safe, respected, and understood. We all want to feel that our skills and perspectives are valued. We all want to play a role in our communities.

The irony is that people who are hungry for this kind of validation are often themselves "conversational narcissists" who are unable to offer the same kind of attention and presence to others that they so wish they had. The result is a vicious circle of superficial connection.

If you wish to be an empathic human being who breaks this cycle, practice first by giving your full attention to the human being in front of you. That means not thinking about what has been said five minutes ago or yesterday, or about what might happen five minutes from now or tomorrow. Think of it as a kind of meditation—every time your mind wanders to yourself or your phone or a judgment on what you're hearing, gently pull it back and simply observe, notice, listen.

Carl Rogers, one of psychology's most famous founding fathers and pioneer of humanist psychology, said that empathic listening is "entering the private perceptual world of the other and becoming thoroughly at home in it" (1980). Get "alongside" the person you're speaking to and become a kind of companion walking with them in their world rather than standing outside of it, passing judgment. Offer silence—but let that silence be alert, alive, and with pricked ears!

Skill 2: Radical Acceptance

First, you **seek to understand. Not judge, appraise, or evaluate.**

As an empathic listener, you temporarily empty yourself of your own need to control the conversation, to be right, or to color the interaction with your own narrative or perceptions. Radically accepting another person's experiential account takes a major paradigm shift. People can find it difficult because they wonder, "Do I really have to accept everything they tell me?"

The answer is yes. But acceptance here goes beyond just agreement or acquiescence. Instead, it means we simply acknowledge and accept *what is* because *it is*. In fact, we realize that **our opinion on the matter is not relevant or necessary—only our awareness and presence is**. If someone confides in us that they've had an abortion and that they now feel like a guilty murderer, the fact that you personally don't think of abortion this way is utterly, entirely irrelevant. *They* do. And all you are doing when you empathize is seeing as far as you possibly can what it means to be them and think this way.

When we validate people this way, we are saying, "You make sense." We look at their interpretation, their account, and their experience of events, and take as a given that this is what is real and true for them. In fact, we don't need to *grant* them this right by listening—their story is complete and sufficient in itself, and our honor is to bear witness to it. The extent to which we accept is the extent to which we pause our own egos and immerse for a moment in theirs.

You may be familiar with a common example: Someone says something like, "I'm such an idiot. I'm never going to get this right," and you jump in, saying, "No way! Don't say that. You're not an idiot." Though it comes from a good place, this response is ultimately based in non-acceptance because it sees the emotional reality . . . and denies it. A more empathic response would be to simply hear and nod, or say, "I can see how frustrated you must feel with it all." (Remember the emotion wheel and labeling?)

If they say they feel like an idiot, well, accept that. Many people think of empathy and compassion as the words you say or the supportive advice you give. But there is immense power in just acknowledging *what is real* because when you do, you send the message: "You are important. How you are feeling has value. I am listening because what you are going through is worthy of attention."

Skill 3: Deep Curiosity

How many of us genuinely find the people around us interesting?

If we're honest, most of us think of ourselves as the center of the universe (understandably) and assume that the shallow surface we encounter in others is all there is to them. When you think about it, this attitude is deeply disrespectful and undermines the dignity and innate value of every person, whoever they are. Being empathic means truly understanding that everybody out there is the center of their own universe. The people you walk by in the street have as rich and complex an inner life as you do, and they are as attached to their joys and sorrows as you are to yours.

Isn't that remarkable? The only way we ever encounter and know one another is when we communicate, reach out, and share. And yet when we do, so many of us waste time on superficialities, boring conventions, and inauthentic personas that hide who we really are.

"Ask questions" is good advice. But don't ask questions simply because you believe it's polite and it makes you seem like you're paying attention. Ask because you genuinely want to bridge the gap between you and the other person. Ask because there's a whole other fascinating and unknown universe inside that person's skull, and you want the privilege of getting to explore it a little. If this concept feels difficult, imagine it from the other side. What would it feel like for someone to genuinely, sincerely want to know about *your* world from the inside out?

Wouldn't it feel liberating and encouraging to have someone truly hear you—without judgment, without interrogating or arguing—and listen to your unique perspective with total openness and interest, even wonder? Well, this kind of deep validation is a gift that we ourselves can offer others any time we listen with empathy.

Ask questions that create space in which the other person can expand. Ask to understand. A question can be like an attack—we can look at something and ask, "What are you and what do you mean?!" as though we are demanding it justify itself to us. But a question can also be a gentle invitation, a soothing caress, a friendly and conversational gesture, or a kindness.

Consider the following questions:

"How do you feel about all this?"

"What happened then?"

"Can you tell me more about X?"

"What do you mean when you say X?"

"How are you making sense of all this?"

"Has this happened before?"

"How did you cope with it?"

"What do you think you want right now?"

"I want to understand—why did X happen?"

Listening is Active!

Beyond the three attitudes described above, there are three main techniques you can use for practicing empathic listening:

1. Mirroring, copying, or repeating
2. Paraphrasing what has been said
3. Reflecting on the emotional content, sometimes with questions or labeling (more on all three of these in a later chapter)

For example, someone is sharing with you some deep concerns about their competency at work.

1. To mirror, you literally repeat what you've been told.
   "I'm such an idiot."
   "An idiot?" Nothing new is added.
2. To paraphrase, you verbally offer the content back to the speaker, but somewhat rephrased to show not just that you've heard, but have comprehended.
   "Seems like you're not confident in your abilities right now."
3. To reflect on emotional content, go a little deeper.

> "Do you think you're feeling a little overwhelmed with the tasks you're given?" The emotion is labeled and reflected back.

Take a look at how the principles of maximum attention, radical acceptance, and deep curiosity play out in the following conversation, and see if you can spot where the listener is using mirroring, paraphrasing, and emotional reflection to show their empathy.

A: Tell me all about it. I know this has been bothering you for a while.

B: Yeah. I don't know, I'm at my wit's end with it all. To tell you the truth, I feel like I have no idea what I'm doing most days. I'm such an idiot.

A: An idiot?

B: Yeah, an idiot! And people are noticing, you know? When they hired me a month ago, they had no idea, clearly.

A: Right. You mean they had no idea that . . . ?

B: Well, that I don't know how to do my job! I actually feel like a fraud. How many more mistakes can I make before they ask me to pack up and leave? I'm dreading it because every day at work could be it.

A: It?

B: Well . . . the day they find out they hired the wrong person.

A: Wow.

B: Look, I don't mean to say I'm a complete idiot— I mean, obviously I do know how to do my job— it's just that . . .

A: (Silence, letting the other person continue, without jumping in to complete their sentence.)

B: It's just that it's a lot all at once, you know?

A: Yeah. It's a lot. Do you think you're feeling a little overwhelmed with all the tasks you're given?

B: Oh, totally. And actually, I don't feel like I can ask for too much help, you know? And I think that's making me pretend I'm coping better with it than I am. But I'm not coping.

Notice how in the above conversation, Speaker A, the listener, has not put any of their own judgment, interpretation, or assumptions into Speaker B's story. But because Speaker A can reflect, ask questions, show interest, and offer respectful silence, Speaker B is actually starting to arrive at their own conclusions about the problem, i.e., that they are feeling overwhelmed and may need to ask for help. It is Speaker B who is gradually coming around to a possible solution, not Speaker A who is suggesting that advice.

Returning to our emotion wheel, Speaker A might have noticed that the initial emotion of anger (anger at the self, that is) is actually covering deeper and more primary emotions of fear and surprise—manifesting as feelings of stress and overwhelm. But rather than outright offering this observation, Speaker A only gently asks, "Do you think . . .?" leaving plenty of room for Speaker B to explain things in their own words, on their own terms.

Take a look at the same conversation conducted without the skills of empathic listening:

A: Tell me all about it. I know this has been bothering you for a while.

B: Yeah. I don't know, I'm at my wit's end with it all. To tell you the truth, I feel like I have no idea what I'm doing most days. I'm such an idiot.

A: Come on, don't say that. That's just your imposter syndrome talking! You're awesome. You got this.

B: Yeah. I know. It's just . . . I don't know. It's just . . .

A: It's just that you have low self-esteem! I get it, I do. I battled low self-esteem for years. Trust me when I say I know it when I see it.

B: Yeah?

A: Oh man, you want to talk about feeling like an idiot, you should have seen me my first year at

Goldman. I was a wreck. I felt like I had a panic attack every morning! I'm not joking. But you've got to meditate. Believe me. Just one day at a time. Mindful, you know? That's the secret.

B: Uh huh.

A: Keep trucking. You'll be fine. I'm proud of you!

B: Thanks.

From the outside, this may seem to many people like a compassionate and friendly conversation . . . but hopefully you can see things with a bit more nuance! Though this Speaker A is well-versed on topics like low self-esteem, imposter syndrome, and the value of mindfulness meditation, they are completely and utterly unable to listen, be present, and accept Speaker B's story with respect and curiosity.

Failing to accept someone's experience is not just about ignoring them or judging them outright; sometimes, we do our most vicious invalidation when we are trying to help by being "positive." You can also see how Speaker A completely steers the conversation toward themselves, giving glib advice and using their own experience as a frame to understand Speaker B's experience. There is even an element of competition ("You think *you* have it bad?").

The story becomes one about low self-esteem, which is not quite what Speaker B is actually experiencing and not the direction they would have steered the conversation if they had felt genuinely listened to. Realizing they are not being heard or understood ("It's just . . . it's just . . ."), Speaker B eventually keeps quiet.

Though Speaker A might have felt that this was a positive and encouraging conversation, the truth is that Speaker B may rightly feel that they can't trust them with their real feelings. The lack of real empathy has made a definite dent to the openness, authenticity, and connection in this relationship. Not to mention, Speaker B is actually no closer to solving their problem—and may even feel that the quick exchange made them feel so much worse ("I can't ask for help or admit that I'm not coping, because then everyone will think I'm not positive/mindful/strong enough. People don't want to hear about it if you're struggling. They just want you to smile and 'keep trucking' . . .").

When someone speaks, listen. For that moment, they are the world's leading expert on their own experience, and you are like a student soaking in the story you're being told. Pay close attention, keep quiet, and take notes!

The Body Can Listen, Too

We've already discussed the value of *verbally* reflecting emotions back to the speaker, but this is just one way that we can practice mirroring in conversations. **Body language can be empathic too, and when your body mirrors another person's, this is a way to show physical "active listening" of the body.**

Let's go back (again) to our ancient ancestors. So-called "limbic synchrony" is about being in sync on a physiological, pre-verbal level. This is the kind of harmony that helped prehistoric groups bond for better survival. Consider that even before babies are born, their heartbeats keep sync with their mothers'. After they're born, mother and baby are closely in tune via a more primal language than words: touch, facial expression, and gesture.

When a little baby smiles, there isn't a human being alive who doesn't immediately smile in return, mirroring that expression. In fact, many psychologists now believe that an infant's sense of self takes shape and matures precisely because of their caregiver's initial response to and reflection of their early experience. We learn to understand ourselves as unique beings, in other words, because other people respond to us as such. We learn that what we are feeling is sadness, for example, because we first see that sadness mirrored back to us in the faces of our caregivers.

Therefore, mirroring and synchrony have deep, ancient roots that speak to the very essence of who we are as human beings. Empathy doesn't just feel nice—it confirms and affirms who we are as human beings. "I see you" on a primal level is no different from "you exist and you matter." This is important.

Keeping emotionally and physically in step with the humans around you is a sign of trust, harmony, connection, and understanding. Many people think of body language as a variant of spoken or verbal expression, but it's more properly the other way around: Evolutionarily speaking, verbal language is a very recent development and an offshoot of our more fundamental ability for *embodied* communication.

This represents a paradigm shift: Listening is not just something you do with your ears, "hearing" someone is about so much more than using your ears, and "seeing" them is, when you think about it, a primarily literal way to witness and comprehend another's "point of view." What's more, the most basic form of comprehension is mimicry—to mirror is to show empathy. What better way to signal that you understand the other person's position than to embody it yourself?

Research has shown that masterful and empathic body language allowed waitresses to earn higher tips (Van Baaren et al., 2003), let salesclerks make bigger sales (Jacob et al., 2011), and allowed women to gain more favorable evaluations from men during a speed dating exercise (Gueguen, 2009). All these people did was consciously or unconsciously copy the

- body language
- attitude and posture
- facial expression
- and vocal qualities

of the people around them.

You're probably wondering, though, *is mirroring always such a good thing*? You've probably experienced awkwardness at realizing that someone was copying you. To minimize weirdness, mirroring has to be done properly. Here's how.

First, make sure that you are **facing the person** square on to signal that they have your complete attention. This builds rapport and trust and sends the message, "You are my focus right now."

Next, be mindful of **eye contact**. You don't want too much or too little, so you can convey attention and interest without being too intense or intrusive. Author and psychologist Dr. Kerstin Uväs-Moberg explains how eye contact actually releases oxytocin, a hormone responsible for fundamental feelings of warmth and closeness.

One thing you might try (although this technique is possibly more suited to professional settings) is to **seek out "yeses."** For example, when you ask questions to which the obvious answer is "yes," you are creating a moment of concurrence and agreement, even if it's only in a very small way. The more you are both nodding and agreeing, even if only on superficial topics, the more you will create a sense of synchrony and being on the same page.

Once you've established some sense of rapport, then you can begin to talk and listen empathically and use body language mirroring. Let's take a look at the kinds of mirroring you could try:

Verbal

Use the words they do. If they are speaking formally, match that. If they are using colorful and creative expressions, meet them there and do the same.

Vocal

This refers to the qualities of the voice itself. If they are speaking quickly, match the pace of their delivery and do the same. Also match their volume (i.e., how loudly or quietly they're speaking, but also the quantity of speech) and, to the extent possible, their pitch (how high or low the voice is). Pay attention to how animated they are being, as well. Is their voice varied and dynamic, changing in pitch and tone and full of expressiveness? Or is it a steady monotone? Are there many pauses, or is it smooth and flowing? This is called cadence. Imagine that a person's voice is almost like a musical genre, and try to reflect back their unique nuances of expression.

Remember that the voice is not something neutral and abstract—it emerges from within our bodies, from the very tissues of our lungs and throat, and is created from the air that we pull in and shape with our lips, tongue, and other muscles. The voice is a deeply personal attribute, and it reflects our emotional and physical state. You might notice that merely by mimicking someone's voice, you also get a firsthand experience of their emotional state. If someone is speaking in a jerky, breathless, and high-pitched voice, speaking like that for just a few moments will not only help you understand their anxiety, but help you *feel* it in your own body!

Postural

If they are sitting very upright, do the same and don't slouch. If they are generally holding their body in a closed, guarded way, do the same. If their gestures are casual and relaxed, match that with your own.

This goes beyond just the immediate posture of the body, though. If someone is giving the impression of being broadly "low energy," for example, you would be felt to be un-empathic if you conducted yourself with extreme enthusiasm and vitality. Think about the attitude and orientation of the *whole* person. You don't need to match that orientation exactly, just harmonize with it.

Idiosyncratic

Everybody has their own unique accent and way of speaking. The same is true for the body. If you pay close attention to how people hold themselves in space, how they move, their gestures, and how they express their physical form, you will start to notice idiosyncrasies—little things that they and only they do. Mirroring these idiosyncrasies can send a powerfully empathic message, sometimes unconsciously.

Maybe they have a habit of quickly lifting an eyebrow at the end of a long sentence. Maybe they have quick hands that get quicker the more excited they become. Maybe they do a certain thing with their tongue or scrunch their shoulders up a little whenever they're feeling embarrassed or awkward. If you mirror these subtle expressions, the other person may suddenly feel deeply understood—without even knowing why!

Be Careful!

Yes, body language is a primal pre-verbal human expression that we all understand without being taught. But that doesn't mean that there aren't certain cultural or contextual facts we need to be mindful of if we want to avoid misunderstandings.

Perhaps it goes without saying that mirroring between a man and a woman will probably need to look a little different from mirroring between two people of the same sex, simply because so many empathic body language signals can easily be interpreted as flirty ones! Likewise, be mindful of any potential role that cultural or even generational differences may play in body language.

Some other words of caution:

- When you mirror, only reflect back the positive and harmonious body language signals. Mirroring things like scowls or crossed arms will only amplify feelings of disharmony.
- Don't be too obvious. A little goes a long way.
- Mirror in a subtle way and then watch to see if the other person is doing the same or pulling back. Then adjust accordingly. If you continue to mirror a person when they've communicated nonverbally that this is *not* welcome, you will likely be

perceived as pushy, insensitive, or boundary-crossing.

When NOT Mirroring is the Empathic Thing to Do

Picture this. Person A has just had an inconclusive test result back from the lab and is now worried that they are seriously ill—potentially with a terminal disease that runs in their family. They are talking to Person B about how desperately anxious they are now; they have to wait till Monday to speak to the consultant, and it's only Friday now. In the absence of knowing any more details, their imaginations are running wild, and they're spiraling deeper and deeper into panic.

Person A paces around the room, face scrunched up in a grimace, hands clenched. They don't seem to know where to put themselves. As they tell Person B all about the scary statistics they read about online, and about their chances of survival if they do have the dreaded disease, Person B notices:

- Their voice is thin and tight, almost like it can't escape the body
- The story is rushed and breathless, delivered in a higher pitch than normal, and rushing along without pause or punctuation. Every single sentence seems to end as a question.

- The mouth and jaw seem tight, and the arms are held clamped against the body

Person B observes and listens for a while. Clearly, Person A is terrified and awash with anxiety. But what they definitely don't want to do here is reflect back the same panic—it would only exacerbate things. In empathy, Person B even starts to feel themselves getting anxious as they listen, but they deliberately take a few deep, slow breaths and consciously choose to do the *opposite* of Person A.

They lower their voice and speak softly, slowing down and giving time for pauses. Instead of delivering a long stream of questions, Person B gives simple, calm statements: "You're panicking right now, I can see that. But the test was inconclusive. That is not the same as bad news. One thing you do know is that you will learn more on Monday..."

Person B does this because over time, Person A will mirror *them*. In a while, Person A does calm down.

Try it next time you're with a very upset or even crying person: Take a deep, obvious breath yourself and deliberately pause, speaking more slowly. You may notice that the other person often does the same. The magical thing is that you can signal support, understanding, and empathy this way, all without saying a word.

Next, Person B gets up and literally takes Person A by the hand, guiding them out the door so that they can go for a walk together. This way, some of the nervous energy is spent on walking, and Person B can demonstrate being physically in sync without being panicked and stressed as well.

If someone is right in the middle of a very strong emotional experience (be it anxiety, depression, shame, or anger), it's usually not a good idea to mirror them. Rather, take note of what their body language is expressing, and with your own body language, gently try to suggest the opposite experience. If they're rushing, speak a little slower than them. If they're shouting, speak with a somewhat lower volume.

Summary

- To listen effectively and empathically, we need to let our egos take a back seat so the other person can lead. If we are sensitive, alert, and respectful, we can listen without an agenda.
- Listen with maximum attention without getting distracted by anything other than the perspective being shared with you in that very moment.
- Seek to understand, not to judge, appraise, or evaluate—in fact, your opinion is irrelevant! Only your presence and awareness are

necessary. Have radical acceptance for what is simply because it is.
- Maintain deep curiosity. Ask questions that create space in which the other person can expand. This sends the message, "You are important. How you are feeling has value. I am listening because what you are going through is worthy of attention and worth knowing more about."
- Use mirroring, paraphrasing, or reflecting to show active listening.
- Body language can be empathic too, and when your body mirrors another person's, this is a way to show physical "active listening" of the body.
- To show that your body is listening, face the person, make comfortable eye contact, and seek to concur with "yeses" or head nods. Then mirror their words, voice, posture, or other idiosyncrasies.
- When mirroring, be mindful of the gender or cultural context, and only reflect what is positive. Avoid mirroring strong negative emotions (panic, anger, depression) and instead model a sense of calm by slowing down and taking a deep breath; the other person may then mirror you.

Chapter 5: Injecting Empathy into Daily Life

Be Still and Reflect

Here is the story of two good friends, Sky and Lake.

One day, Lake asked Sky, "What's it like to be you?"

Sky thought about it for a moment and then created a few impressively shaped clouds.

"Like *this*," said Sky.

Lake went very quiet and still until his surface was like a mirror. In a few moments, the clouds that Sky had made were perfectly reflected on the surface of Lake.

"Ah, I see what you mean!" said Lake.

When we listen empathically and reflect, what we are doing is going quiet and still

within ourselves so we can receive as accurate a picture of the other person's account as possible. Then, we can hold up that same account and show it back to the speaker, asking, "Is this right? Is this what you meant?"

And in the same way that a lake has to be free of ripples and waves to accurately reflect the sky, we need to be still and free from our own mental noise, prejudice, and ego to properly receive and reflect the narrative someone else is sharing.

In our little story, the lake and the sky reflect each other so well that they are actually showing one another the same image. In a truly empathic connection, people can likewise feel that they "get" one another, that they are on the same wavelength, and that there is a real sense of in-tune *conversation* going on.

If you think about it, the only one who can say whether you've been empathic or not is the person you're listening to. Only they can confirm whether you have actually understood them. So why not ask? Well, reflecting is a way to check that you have in fact heard. Being empathic and kind doesn't mean we have to be psychic, after all!

When you reflect an accurate picture to the speaker, you convey empathy because you are essentially saying, "I see what you mean!" but also, "Is this what you mean?"

You are providing them with that precious sense of being seen, validated, and understood. You show that you're listening and that you care, and that feels good. It strengthens a feeling of trust and connection and helps *you* become a better and more humble conversationalist. With reflective, empathic listening, you are inviting the other person to have a more authentic, more connected relationship with you, and asking them to teach you about what they need. It also helps you avoid potential misunderstandings or hurt feelings.

Psychologist Dr. Ann Vertel uses reflective listening in her practice and says if you "reflect back to someone what they are feeling, you meet them right where they are emotionally. You've connected with them; they don't feel quite so alone with this feeling."

But that's not all reflective listening can be used for. When you reflect, you may very well help the other person to better understand their own emotional experiences. By receiving, focusing, and reflecting what you're told, you show them aspects they might not have seen before—or simply validate what they haven't felt confident enough to admit they already know. In other words, by attempting to gain more clarity, you invite them to do the same. As you articulate their experience, they learn to better articulate it for themselves. What a gift to share with someone you care about!

How to Master Reflective Listening

Reflecting is:

- Paraphrasing and restating all parts of a speaker's message back to them
- Allowing the speaker to "hear" what their own story sounds like
- Demonstrating your willingness to understand
- A way to encourage the speaker to keep speaking, and maybe even solve problems

Reflecting is not:

- Asking questions
- Starting a new thread or introducing a new topic
- Leading, shaping, or dominating the conversation in any way

We've already encountered two great ways to reflect in the previous section: **mirroring** and **paraphrasing**.

To mirror, we repeat the literal word or phrase we've heard. To mirror well, keep it short and sweet and don't do too much—mirroring is just the start and is not enough on its own.

A: "So I looked him square in the eye and I said no."

B: "You said no."

A: "Damn right I did."

To paraphrase, you use words with the same meaning to show your comprehension.

A: "So I looked him square in the eye and I said no."

B: "You totally refused!"

A: "I sure did."

Be careful here, though, not to introduce your own ideas or distort the speaker's meaning:

A: "So I looked him square in the eye and I said no."

B: "Oh no, you rejected him!"

Whether you are mirroring, paraphrasing, or a mix of both, the key is to be **non-judgmental and non-directional**—i.e., get your ego out the way! Questions have their place, but they should ideally come sometime *after* the speaker has confirmed that your understanding is correct, and that you are both broadly on the same page. Your questions should never feel like they come with an agenda.

To develop your reflective listening skills, it's worth understanding *what* exactly you're reflecting. You can reflect:

1. Content
2. Feeling
3. Meaning

Or all three.

Let's consider an example.

A close friend is opening up to you about her difficulties with dating a man more than ten years older than her. She tells you about a hurtful occasion when her partner declined to spend Christmas together because he was spending it with his children from a previous marriage. What's worse, he ignored several messages and spent the day coordinating with the ex-wife, forgetting to wish your friend a Merry Christmas. When your friend brought up the issue with him, he was confused and eventually hostile—did he expect her to put his own kids second? Now, your friend is extremely upset. As you talk to her, you reflect back her story, but on several levels:

Content – the factual information, events, and actions that have been shared—for example, the fact that your friend has never met her partner's kids but has been seeing him for many years.

Feeling – the emotional material behind what you're being told. Why is your friend upset? She might be feeling side-lined, undermined, or put in a difficult position. She may be feeling jealous, left out, undervalued, or even suspicious.

Meaning – Reading between the lines, you pick out what this episode means for your friend: She may conclude that this means she's not as important a person in her partner's life as he is in hers, and she feels rejected. The events mean, in her world, that she is not number one to her partner.

As you reflect her story back to her, you may start by confirming the more factual content and gradually move to the emotional content, finally reflecting what the ultimate meaning of the story/experience is (sometimes, this will be as much as a revelation to the speaker as it is to you!). Even better, see if you can link the content with the emotional or meaning elements.

For example,

"I mean, I'm not crazy to think that after two years, I should have met his children by now, right?"

"Do you think you feel a little left out?"

Note in the above example that the question being asked is not literally looking for confirmation that the speaker isn't crazy, but something more subtle than this—a validation of the hurt they feel. The question, then, is not about the factual content (after how many years should you meet your partner's children from a previous marriage?) and more about the emotion and meaning behind these facts. If you had merely stayed on the superficial and factual level, the speaker would not have felt as validated:

"I mean, I'm not crazy to think that after two years, I should have met his children by now, right?"

"My cousin never met her guy's kids until they had been dating for like five years, so it's not unusual."

"Oh."

When we listen empathically and reflect back someone's emotional experience to them, it can sometimes feel like we are taking a bunch of different pieces and putting them all together in a more understandable order before handing it all back to them. If you are very empathic and listen well, people may tell you at the end of a conversation, "Thank you so much for helping me figure that out; you're completely right!" Of course, you haven't done anything but reflect—*they* are the ones who have found insight into the situation because of the coherent picture you reflected back to them.

There is no step-by-step guide to help you master reflective listening—how could there be when the other person is guiding it all and the conversation is emerging organically? But there are a few things to keep in mind. Remember, also, that practice makes perfect. If you get something completely wrong, that's not a problem—just an opportunity to reiterate your interest in getting it right. The emotion and meaning behind your actions will be registered even if you're inaccurate on the details/content.

- Slow down, relax, and be natural. Nobody is in a therapy chair, and there are no prizes or report cards. While you're busy not judging them, don't judge yourself either.
- As you're told facts and details, try to listen for the emotion and meaning behind them. ("He spent the day with his ex but couldn't send me a single text?") What is the possible emotion here? What does this *mean* for the person in front of you?
- Proceed gradually. Don't dive in with the deep and heavy stuff. Take your time and let them set the pace.
- When you paraphrase or mirror, check to see how the image is received. Ask, "Have I understood?" or simply be alert to a nod, a smile, or any other body language clues.
- If someone uses a very pointed metaphor or image, use the same one as they do, and even keep it going ("It's like he has these two sides to him, and I'm only allowed to know one side. I feel like a fool." "Do you think you feel like a fool because you've shared your full self with him?").

- Imagine yourself as an "emotional highlighter"—when you hear someone speak, pay close attention to emotions or implied emotions so that when you reflect back, your understanding contains the most important emotional aspects. If you merely reflect back, "Your partner didn't wish you Merry Christmas," you give a truthful account but not the full account.
- Be careful when making links and associations. If you tie together facts, feelings, and meaning and present them to the speaker, they may feel profoundly heard and understood—but if you've made sweeping assumptions, you might cause offense. Rearrange the material given to you, but *don't add anything extra*—especially not your own biases, fears, or assumptions. ("I guess I feel left out." "I get it. It can be hard feeling like a man's leaving you on the shelf.")

Psychologizing—A Peculiar Kind of Invalidation

Before we conclude this chapter, it's worth taking a look at a conversational phenomenon that is seldom noticed and called out for what it is—psychologizing. When you psychologize, you understand and analyze complex human situations in (sometimes reductive) psychological terms. Psychology is a specific, non-neutral set of assumptions; it is composed of a collection of various models, but that's all they are—models. And all models are necessarily flawed.

These models and the assumptions they take for granted are now commonplace for everyone, not just those in the mental health professions. A strange side-effect of increased mental-health awareness also means that the public sphere is awash in terms that used to be reserved for professionals, such as *trauma*, *anxiety*, *narcissistic*, *obsessive*, and so on.

When we intend to be empathic listeners, we may unconsciously start acting the role of a therapist or psychologist. We immediately engage in a kind of listening behavior we assume is standard practice, and this means *interpreting* the experiences of ourselves and others in psychological terms. The only trouble is, this can be precisely the thing that makes us terrible listeners! **When we are interpreting, we are no longer listening. We are no longer genuinely reflecting.**

Imagine a friend tells you about an experience they had. They explain how they were camping one day in the mountains and had a mind-blowing religious experience where they encountered the spirit of their deceased grandmother, who told them that she was safe and sound on the other side. You listen with care and empathy, and then say, "Well, it was probably a dream. Dreams can reveal our unconscious desires," and, "It must have been so traumatic to lose your grandmother. The brain will make up all sorts of things as a coping mechanism!"

These explanations, to put it bluntly, are wrong. That's because your friend *did not* have a psychological experience. They had a spiritual/religious one. When we empathize, we enter into the *whole* world of the other person—and that really means their whole world, including all their epistemological assumptions, their philosophical framework, and how they see the very universe and their place in it.

Sometimes, when we are too quick to look for psychological explanations, or when we try to squeeze living breathing people into archetypes or popular theories, we invalidate how they understand themselves. And empathy vanishes. If you find yourself readily announcing that certain people are psychopaths or narcissists, if you accuse people in arguments of projecting, if you call someone else's opinion a bias (but your own is a preference), and if you mock those who disagree with you as having unresolved childhood issues, then realize that you are using psychology as a weapon.

In our attempt to reflect, we may give back a picture that is heavily tinted by the (flawed) concepts of psychology, and this may do damage to the people we're trying to encounter authentically and spontaneously. If you recognize some of yourself in this, try to counter the tendency by imagining that every person you talk to is actually a theoretical outlier—a person who doesn't fit any mold at all. In other words, if you must use a psychological frame, imagine that every person gets *their own* completely unique and tailor-made model that's just for them . . . and that it's up to them to tell you about this model, not for you to tell them!

One of the best ways to cure yourself of the psychologizing habit is to really notice how bad it feels when people do it to you. Is it *really* helpful to have someone reflect back a psychological theory about your deeply personal, sensitive, emotional experiences? Wouldn't you rather have them just listen, treat you like the individual you are, and hear what you say without analyzing it?

Banish psychological jargon from your vocabulary, and whatever you do, don't start sentences with, "Well, Jung once said . . ." or "according to the early behaviorists . . ." Refrain from trying to "explain" people's behaviors to them or justify the present by looking to childhood or to the unconscious mind. Most of the time, this feels pretty invalidating. After all, people don't want to be examined; they want to be supported, valued, heard, and appreciated. They are not stereotypical examples in a psych textbook, but unique people experiencing all the joys and sorrows of life.

If your friend says they had a religious experience and met the spirit of their dead grandmother on the mountain, then that's exactly what happened. Likewise, if your great aunt tells you she is a "tomboy," don't invalidate that description by diagnosing her from your armchair with "gender dysphoric disorder"!

Be Curious

We explored curiosity earlier and saw how listening, paying attention, and asking meaningful questions are all manifestations of an attitude of curiosity. Let's look closer.

Without curiosity, empathy isn't possible.

Have you ever been in conversation with someone who threw question after question at you but didn't make much of an effort to actually listen to your answers? Have you ever had someone *say* they understand what you're feeling when you can tell they don't understand at all?

Curiosity is about more than asking questions or saying the right words—it's about having a sincere desire to understand someone else's heart, mind, and complete

experience. If you've ever been on the receiving end of fake interest or attention that was given out of a sense of politeness or duty, you'll know that when it comes to empathy, the curiosity has to be **genuine**.

In this chapter, we'll look at some concrete techniques and approaches to cultivate deeper curiosity for those around us... however, it's not really a question of technique, but of mindset. Real curiosity is like an existential orientation. It's what allows us to be enthralled by the unknown, to be drawn toward something unfamiliar to us, and to open respectfully and with inquisitiveness to something that is outside our normal range of perception.

If you wonder about what is going on in someone else's head (curiosity), you have already gone halfway to reaching out to them, understanding them, and responding with compassion (empathy). When we are a little too comfortable in our own narrow and automatic assumptions about life, it can take a conscious effort to let that all go and instead dig a little deeper to what lies under the surface.

It requires imagination—*What is it really like to be a completely different person than the one I am?*

And it requires a hunger to know and a determination to dig for a richer comprehension—*WHY did this person do such-and-so? What does it mean to them?*

Finally, it requires an open mind—*Can I put my own fixed beliefs and ideas aside and immerse in theirs? Can I just observe without judgment or evaluation?*

Take a look at this conversation:

A: "My parents were entering me in beauty pageants since before I could walk. That was when we still lived in China. All my life, I've been taught to focus on my appearance, so now that I'm getting a bit older, I realize that I'm terrified of aging. But it's not a vanity thing—I think I genuinely don't know how to engage with people as someone who's ... well, *not* pretty, you know?"

B: "I know exactly what you mean."

It seems pretty empathic on the surface, but if B is a middle-aged professional man who's never given a thought to his appearance, it is highly unlikely that he does know what A means. How could he? Here, empathy is offered but without curiosity—Person A may feel like they've been cut short or given an obligatory platitude that doesn't really mean anything. Instead, consider this conversation:

A: "My parents were entering me in beauty pageants since before I could walk. That was when we still lived in China. All my life, I've been taught to focus on my appearance, so now that I'm getting a bit older, I realize that I'm terrified of aging. But it's not a vanity thing—I think I genuinely don't know how to engage with people as someone who's ... well, *not* pretty, you know?"

B: "Woah, beauty pageants since before you could walk? How does that even work?"

A: "Well, you know, baby pageants and things! It's kind of crazy."

B: "I see. I guess I always thought that that kind of thing was an American phenomenon. Is it popular over there?"

A: "No, not hugely popular . . . but I think it's becoming more popular."

B: "So if you're involved in that from the time you're a baby . . . I'm just trying to understand what that must feel like. What did your parents tell you? Like, how did they explain what was happening?"

A: "I know, it's pretty weird. But that's exactly it—when you're young, you just go with it. It took me a long time to realize that that was not normal."

B: "I'm trying to imagine how it was like for you. Were you there as a toddler, thinking, *I hope I look pretty enough*? Is that how it was?"

A: "Kind of. It was more a feeling of not wanting to disappoint my parents, I think. Even as a very young kid, you can feel that expectation. It's hard to explain."

B: "Oh, I'm sure. But I think I know exactly what you mean."

In this case, Person B may sincerely know what Person A means; even though they cannot begin to imagine what the world of Chinese child beauty pageants is like, they do know how it feels to be pressured by parents. After a few genuinely curious questions and open-minded listening, by the time Person B says, "I know exactly what you mean," Person A is likely to believe it.

When we are curious, we are open-mindedly observing what is in front of us and gathering as much information as possible. Whereas empathy is the message, "How you feel matters to me," curiosity sends the message, "I want to really, truly understand how you feel."

The main thing that gets in the way of real curiosity in empathic listening is the impulse to insert our own opinion, perspective, or frame of reference into the conversation. Notice how Person B in the above conversation doesn't launch into a speech about their own feelings toward child beauty pageants, and they also don't run off on a tangent about what they know of this phenomenon in America. They don't share an experience of that one time they entered the school talent competition, or about their views on a documentary they watched last year about eating disorders.

They simply listen and ask questions.

Brian Grazer is the author of the bestseller *A Curious Mind: The Secret to a Bigger Life*. He says, "We are all trapped in our own way of thinking. Trapped in our own way of relating to people. We get so used to seeing the world our own way, we come to think that the world is the way that we see it."

It's so easy to dismiss the perspectives of other people in favor of our own. If you have difficulty caring about other people's perspectives, however, remind yourself that empathic conversation is a brilliant **opportunity**—a chance to peek outside the limits of your own skull and learn something that you could never teach yourself. Learning to be interested in others is not a boring challenge, but a gift. Understanding this will allow you to make the mindset shift into being a genuinely curious and empathic listener.

You will know that you've made the shift because when you are curious, you will witness that people almost seem to "bloom" in your presence. When you behold another person with openness and an inquiring, receptive mind, you invite them to be themselves. You give them permission to express their reality. What's more, you encourage them to be curious about their own mental states. Sometimes, your questions can be the very catalyst to inspiring a certain mindset shift in them. In this way, curiosity combined with empathy doesn't just create good vibes and connection—it can solve problems, kindle creativity, and shine light on new, unexplored insights.

In his book *Curious: The Desire to Know and Why Your Future Depends on It*, author Ian Leslie says,

> "The true beauty of learning stuff, including apparently useless stuff, is that it takes us out of ourselves, reminds us that we are part of a far greater project, one that has been underway for at least as long as human beings have been talking to each other. Other animals don't share or store their knowledge like we do. Orangutans do not reflect on the history of the orangutan; London's pigeons have not adopted ideas on navigation from pigeons in Rio de Janeiro. We should all feel privileged to have access to a deep well of species memory. As comedian Stephen Fry suggests, it's foolish not to take advantage of it."

Three Types of Curiosity

Let's take a closer look at what we mean when we say a person is curious. According to Leslie, there are three broad types.

Type 1: Diversive Curiosity

This refers to being attracted to novelty. Whenever we're inspired to explore new places, new food, or new activities, it's usually this type of curiosity driving us. It's a kind of beginner's feeling, though, and is usually just the igniting spark that begins a more thorough investigation.

Type 2: Epistemic Curiosity

Epistemology is the philosophical branch of inquiry related to the theory of knowledge itself. In other words, it's about gaining knowledge and how we gain knowledge—where it comes from, what it looks like, its limits, and so on. Naturally, this is curiosity pitched at a much deeper level than the mere thrill of novelty, and is much more structured and directed than the open-ended desire to ask, "What's this?"

Epistemic curiosity requires conscious effort and work—It can be a challenge to question and analyze the very foundation you are standing on when you ask those questions!

Type 3: Empathic Curiosity

The type we are interested in here. This is the ability to consciously inquire into someone else's lived experience. Their thoughts, feelings, and perceptions. In a way, it is not unlike epistemic curiosity, where we delve deeply into the rules on which the philosophy of knowledge is run. But in the case of empathic curiosity, we are narrowing our focus to one specific individual. What is the world they live in, and what are its organizing principles? How is meaning structured in their universe, and on what beliefs (laws) is it ordered?

To demonstrate the difference between these three, imagine that you meet a new person at a party and start talking to them.

Diversive curiosity makes you wonder things like, "Hm, I wonder if he's single," or, "I wonder where she got that awesome T-shirt from."

Epistemic curiosity might make you ask questions like, "I wonder if we could ever see eye to eye, her being a Scientologist and all . . ." or, "I wonder what he thinks of me."

Empathic curiosity shows up in questions like, "I wonder *why* she chose Scientology in the first place," or, "I wonder what it's like sincerely believing in a religion that so many people happily mock."

Here's an exercise to try: The next time you find yourself in diversive curiosity, see if you can challenge yourself to find some further empathic curiosity for the subject at hand. Every time you idly think, "I wonder why . . ." follow that thought and see where it takes you!

To be excellent listeners, we need to show curiosity, but it also needs to be a deep and more sophisticated form of curiosity than being idly interested in something a little new or unusual. For example, your new date may be "curious" about you, but there's a big difference between wanting to know what makes you tick as a human being, and just being nosy about what you look like naked!

Keep the Spark of Curiosity Alive

Most of the strategies we explore in this book are best practiced with real people out there in the real world. But curiosity is a personal characteristic that you can develop on your own, knowing that it will indirectly benefit every social connection in your life. In fact, relationships aren't the only thing that will improve with a hearty dose of curiosity—if you can maintain an open mind and a receptive attitude, expect to feel more creative, more optimistic, more inspired, and more resilient in every area of your life.

The good news is that you were *born* curious. It's your birth right as a human being! All you need to do is put some kindling on that fire. Here are some ways to flex the curiosity muscle, and what that might look like when extended to your connections with others.

Focus on WHY

"Why" is like a powerful pickaxe that lets you dig right down to the deep and meaningful stuff. As children, it seems like we ask why once a minute, but as adults, we stop—maybe because we wrongly assume we already know the answer. Asking why is a humble, fearless act—humble because it acknowledges that we don't know everything, and fearless because we're willing to face the unknown. Ask big whys, but ask small ones too (hint: sometimes it's the smallest ones that turn into the biggest!).

Imagine your mother-in-law gave you an item for your new baby, but the baby has now outgrown it, so you say you'll sell the item since it's no longer needed. The mother-in-law angrily demands the gift back, and you're hurt—isn't it *yours*? Your own perspective tells you that it's utterly rude to ask for a gift back, but in empathy and curiosity, you understand that this is not your mother-in-law's perspective.

Instead of arguing, you ask sincerely "Why?" What does it mean to her? You realize that the item has sentimental value, and that in selling it, it would be as if she was no longer needed in the child's life. By holding on to the gift, she feels that she is getting to preserve a very meaningful part of the child's life for posterity. It all makes sense to you, and you can now act empathically.

<u>Try it yourself</u>: The next time you're angry with someone or can't understand their actions, ask WHY. Not why from *your* perspective, but from *theirs*. You might be surprised by the empathy you're then capable of.

Resist Superficiality

Sadly, in our digital age, we are seldom encouraged to be deep, subtle thinkers, but to instead skim over complexity, make snap judgments based on sound bites and sensationalist headlines, and smooth over nuance with lazy assumptions. But this is not what life is really like, and it's not what *people* are like.

The internet gives us all a false sense of knowledge—we glide over the shallow superficialities and, when things get difficult or complex, we skip along to the next thing, never really challenging ourselves or staying with one idea to explore it in the depth it deserves. In other words, our attention spans are short. And it makes us feel that we know more about any one phenomenon than we actually do.

This translates to how we deal with one another. We look at a complicated, multi-faceted human being and reduce them to a few simple stereotypes. She's a liberal feminist type. He's one of those crypto currency guys. They are homeschooling their kids—and you know what *that* means, right?

Judgment kills empathy. Assumptions kill curiosity.

Right now, you could probably think of things about yourself that don't fit "the mold." Maybe you're a mom of seven, but maybe you're also a world-renowned bioethicist who is a key architect in your country's health policies. Maybe you have a body full of tattoos, a garage full of custom Harleys . . . and a flourishing Etsy business where you sell handsewn dog costumes. You get the idea—people are complex. If you are, then so are others. Commit to finding out how *they* don't fit the mold, either. Assume that people will surprise you, and they often do!

<u>Try it yourself</u>: Think of someone you know or have just met. Ask yourself what you are assuming about them. Then, simply turn this into a question instead so that it doesn't shut down the discovery process, but inspires it. For example, instead of just thinking to yourself, "This guy is an evangelical Christian. I bet he's probably a bit weird about gay people . . ." turn that into a genuine question. "So, I'm curious, what is your church's position on homosexuality? I hope that's not a rude question, but I've been genuinely wondering about it . . ."

Authentic curiosity and interest will almost always be welcome, but you may also be surprised to learn that your knee-jerk assumptions are completely unfounded. "Well, people are pretty tolerant. To be honest, I grew up atheist and gravitated to the church only a few years ago, and they were very accepting. Oh, uh, I'm gay, by the way."

No Such Thing as Boring

When you're a kid, you can be held in rapt attention by a soap bubble, a bug on a leaf, or someone pulling a funny face. Try to recapture that same sense of finding **everything** interesting. Because it is! Here's a secret: Things often seem boring precisely because we're not paying attention to them. Think about that: **It is our intense interest and curiosity that transforms the world we behold.**

Artist and composer John Cage gives this advice: "If something is boring after two minutes, try it for four. If still boring, then eight. Then sixteen. Then thirty-two. Eventually one discovers that it is not boring at all."

When you are curious, there is no such thing as a boring person or a boring story. Nothing is so irrelevant that it doesn't warrant your respectful attention. If you delve beneath the surface and uncover the connections between things, then you cannot help but see *everything* as brimming with significance.

Think of something you find uninteresting—postage stamps or tax law. Challenge yourself to dig a little deeper and find something interesting about it. For instance, an ultra-rare British Guiana one-cent magenta stamp fetched £5.6 million at a New York auction in 2014. Even more interesting still, the stamp's previous owner had died in prison four years earlier after being charged and convicted for the murder of an Olympic wrestling champion, of all things.

Did you know that for some countries, the money made from selling stamps to stamp collectors actually exceeds revenue from ordinary postal needs—in fact, some countries produce stamps that have no ordinary postal use at all but are printed exclusively for stamp collectors. In 2013, Belgium created a chocolate-flavored stamp, and Bhutan made a famous 1973 stamp that could play the national anthem if set carefully on a record player . . .

<u>Try it yourself:</u> The next time you're bored, challenge yourself to *make* what you're encountering interesting. Keep asking why. At the very least, ask, "Why does this person find this idea so interesting?" You might not, but isn't it noteworthy that *they* do?

Random Acts of Kindness

Hopefully, you are beginning to see that cultivating a mindset of kindness, compassion, and true empathy is far, far more than just familiarity with a set of tricks and techniques. Being empathic is about being still (i.e., getting our own ego and biases out of the way), being reflective, and being curious. But it's also, at a very basic level, about kindness. Think about the reason you picked up this book in the first place—deep down, you probably shared that noble instinct that belongs to all humans: the instinct to serve, to help, to share, to love, and to be kind.

Sure, you may have the goal of becoming a better listener and enriching your own personal relationships. **But the irony of being more empathic is that it is a goal that's *purely for other people's benefit*. It's a kind of giving that you do without the expectation of being rewarded.** In other words, you want to be a better listener and more engaging conversationalist not so that people will like you and think you're charming, but so that people will feel good (of course, you may well get all those other benefits as a side effect . . .).

In this chapter, we'll be looking at a powerful and effective way to help shape a more empathic mindset. You can change how you behave in the world by changing your mindset, but you can also change your mindset by changing how you act in the world. If you have enough discipline to regularly apply yourself to the task of being kind to others every day, you can't help but grow in empathy and warmth. Empathy is the basis for kindness... but being kind *first* can also kindle the fires of empathy.

You may be surprised to discover that the more you volunteer, give to charity, and help out, the easier it is to listen, reflect, and empathize with people on a more abstract level. In essence, it's a "fake it before you make it" strategy: You are acting as though you are an empathic person even if you don't quite have the full mindset just yet. It doesn't matter, because in time, you will. Your empathy will grow with each kind action. And the more your empathy grows, the more sincere those actions will become.

Kindness is a quality of the soul. It's a spirit of wanting to be helpful for its own sake.

When you are kind and charitable, though, something else happens: You expose yourself to people who are less fortunate than yourself. By immersing a little in their reality, you start to gain a different perspective on your own—congratulations! Not only does this help you foster more genuine understanding of other people's pain, but it will give you a more rounded look on your own assumptions, biases, and blind spots.

When we are kind, we feel better, the other person feels better, and we release a sense of positivity out into the world. Those people are then more likely to be kind, and our actions ripple out. When we listen with kind and non-judgmental attention to someone, they are all the more able to consider *themselves* with the same care and respect, as well as carry that generous mindset to everyone else they encounter.

Okay, so what does "be kind" actually look like? Well, the world is your oyster! Here are some ideas to get you started:

- If you're in line at a coffee shop, offer to pay for the person behind you.
- When you're walking in the street, smile warmly at people who pass you by.
- Challenge yourself to give someone a (genuine) compliment every day.
- Scroll through your contacts list and see who you haven't spoken to in a while. Then, pick three people to reach out to. Tell them something to make them smile, ask how they're doing, or even consider giving them a gift or posting them a handwritten letter.
- Pass on any unused coupons, gift cards with a remaining balance, or parking tickets that still have time on them. Leave a little change in the vending machine or at the laundromat. What you don't really

need may make a world of difference to someone in a pinch.
- Give your home a much-needed tidy up while at the same time putting together a box of items to go to the charity store. If you haven't used it in more than a year, you won't miss it, yet it may be sorely needed by someone else.
- Create spontaneous good vibes in your neighborhood. Form a heart shape out of stones on your daily walk in the woods, leave an inspiring handwritten poem on someone's windshield, write "you're doing great" in the beach sand, or tie a flower onto a stop sign with a ribbon.
- Take a moment to create a few care packages, including non-perishable food, warm socks and gloves, and a few treats. Go out on a cold morning and hand them to the first homeless people you meet.
- Offer someone your seat on the bus or train—they don't have to be elderly or pregnant, either!
- At work, think about two people in your network who don't know each other, but who may benefit from meeting. Introduce them—you could start something wonderful.
- Keep track of people's birthdays and make sure that you always send good wishes. For many people, birthdays are

especially hard, and they may feel completely forgotten.
- Think carefully about the ideas or issues in the world that most speak to your heart. Then, ask yourself what you could be doing to make a difference in that area. Seek out volunteer opportunities or explore ways that your resources, expertise, or simply your presence could be put to good use.
- Spare a thought for the people who have been kind to *you*. Is it maybe time to reach out and show your gratitude to them? Is there someone you've been taking for granted?
- Consider this: Forgiveness is also an act of kindness. If someone has done you wrong and you feel legitimately upset, consciously decide to let it go instead.
- Charity starts at home. Pay attention to what is going on with your neighbors and in your community. Can you walk someone's dog, help out with a lift, donate a dinner, or step in to do emergency childcare?
- Keep elderly folk in your thoughts. Show them your appreciation by seeking their advice or asking them to teach you something or share a skill. These days, we all run to Google, but in the past, we treated elders as a source of knowledge and wisdom. Consulting someone in this

way (even if it's just to ask for a recipe or get advice on stain removal) is a great way to show kindness—and may be appreciated far more than trying to help *them*!
- Consider joining a charity where you can act as a Big Brother or Big Sister for a child who needs mentorship and guidance.
- Help animals—yes, our empathy doesn't have to be limited to humans! It matters even if all you do is rescue an ant from drowning or put out a dish of water and some food for the backyard strays. Animals are excellent teachers of empathy because they are nonverbal and challenge us to pay attention to raw, unmediated experience, not to the superficial.
- Give anonymously. In empathy, we may notice that to be the recipient of our charity is sometimes made uncomfortable, and this brings up feelings of shame, or else changes the social dynamic in tricky ways. So, give someone the gift of not knowing who helped them. It brings a little magic, wonder, and gratitude into the world—and keeps your ego out of it!

You can probably think of many, many more ideas for ways to bring kindness to both those closest to you and to those you don't even know.

But as you try some of them, you may realize that the best actions are those that arise spontaneously from a genuine feeling of generosity within you. They are also the kind of acts that are *responsive*—they emerge in the very moment when another person's need is greatest.

For this, you need to be aware of other people and their needs. One way to strengthen this awareness is to **continually ask yourself, "How are other people doing right now**?" You can do this when you wake up in the morning, or you can do it spontaneously in any social interaction as it unfolds. This awareness of and sensitivity to other people's emotional states and needs are the foundation for genuine empathy (plus, it prevents us from doing that kind of "help" that the other person doesn't actually want or need . . .).

For example, you notice that a colleague at work is having an extremely hard time juggling their schedule and childcare duties. Being aware that they have a deadline coming up, you step in and finish up their work for them while they tend to an emergency at home. Knowing that they already feel on edge about it all, you don't offer and make a big show of your charity. You just do it and save them the trouble.

Maybe you notice a man in a wheelchair having difficulty with his dog's leash. You step in quickly and help him untangle it, giving him a warm smile before you walk off again.

Or perhaps you remember that this time last year, your friend's mother passed away. You give them a little extra love and attention, offering to take them out if they like, knowing they might appreciate the distraction and to be spoiled a little by a friend who cares.

As you can see, all of the above examples rest on your awareness of another person's needs. When you are getting the hang of being kind and empathic, you do much less planning and scheming, and far more *responding* to people's emerging needs in the moment. This ability to be tuned into other people's realities (rather than your own idea of what you think helping them should look like) is what characterizes a genuinely generous heart.

The more you give in this way, the more you shape yourself into someone who is not just being empathic here and there, but who is really *living* an attitude of kind receptivity day after day. One of the biggest mindset shifts, then, is to go from asking the questions, "How can I be a kinder person? How can I be a better listener? How can I improve myself by being more compassionate?" to asking the questions, "Who around me needs help? What is that person thinking and feeling? What is it like to experience life from their point of view?"

See the difference? Kindness, then, is about the shift from the focus on the self to the focus on the other.

Summary

- When we listen empathically and reflect, we go quiet and still within ourselves so we can receive as accurate a picture of the other person's account as possible. We use mirroring and paraphrasing without questioning, leading, or starting a new thread.
- We can reflect either content, feeling, or meaning, but should always remain non-directional and non-judgmental.
- Avoid psychologizing. When we interpret people's experiences, we are no longer fully listening to them.
- Empathy is impossible without curiosity. Curiosity is about more than asking questions—it's about having a sincere desire to understand someone else's heart, mind, and complete experience. It requires imagination, a hunger to learn, and an open mind.
- The main thing that gets in the way of real curiosity in empathic listening is the impulse to insert our own opinion, perspective, or frame of reference into the conversation. Imagine that learning to be interested in others is not a boring challenge, but a gift and an opportunity.

- There are three kinds of curiosity: diversive (interest in novelty), epistemic (deeper inquiry into knowledge itself), and empathic. Whenever you notice mild interest in novelty, see if you can explore and amplify it till it becomes richer empathic curiosity.
- Keep the spark of curiosity alive by consistently asking why, digging beneath the superficiality of a situation, and challenging yourself to see nothing as boring.
- Random acts of kindness can make us more empathic. Try to be more alert to other people's needs and respond spontaneously to them.
- Kindness is a shift from focus on the self to focus on the other. Continually ask yourself, "How are other people doing? What do they need?"

Chapter 6: Empathic Communication is the Ultimate Goal

The Power of Empathic Statements

Stephen Covey, well-loved author of bestseller *The 7 Habits of Highly Effective People*, says that when we communicate, we should "first seek to understand, then to be understood." Similarly, when communicating empathically with others, we should **first listen, then speak.** In the previous section, we explored how we can use words to reflect back the speaker's emotional reality, which shows support, validation, and a perspective on the problem they may not have seen before. But of course, at some point, you're going to want to say something a bit more!

Words can be powerful. When people are upset, we need to pay special attention to how we verbally validate their experience, encourage them, and show our empathy—easier said than done!

Before we begin, let's reiterate the difference between **sympathy** and **empathy**.

Having sympathy means feeling pity for someone else's misfortune. It means feeling sorry for them (note, these are feelings *you* experience in response to someone else's situation).

Having empathy, however, means understanding *their* feelings. It is a question of perspective-taking and of feeling *with* someone rather than standing outside their experience, looking in and being aware only of your own emotional response to it.

Sympathy can increase the distance between people; empathy can shorten it.

What to Say, What Not to Say

Renowned shame researcher and author Brene Brown says, "Rarely can a response make something better; what makes something better is connection." This means that if we're ever talking to someone and unsure if what we're about to say will help, we can ask whether it comes from a place of acknowledging their emotions (empathy), or if it's simply a reflection of our own (sympathy). We can ask whether what we say creates more or less emotional connection.

Take a look at a few things to avoid saying.

Avoid Deflecting

In other words, turning the conversation away from the difficult or painful thing that has just been shared. People can do this because they feel uncomfortable with the emotions shared, or uncomfortable with their own ability to do anything to help. This awkwardness is their emotion, however, and in letting it lead, the other person can feel embarrassed, alone, and even insulted.

Examples:

A: "I've had the worst day of my life. I just want to get in bed and never get out again ..."

B: "Woah, that, uh ... that sounds rough. By the way, did you remember to pick up milk?"

A: "After she said that, I've never been the same again, to be honest."

B: "I'm sorry to hear that. Women, huh! Are you getting the next round?"

A: "Sometimes, I wonder what it's all about, you know? Like, would anyone actually care if I wasn't here anymore...?"

B: "Yeah." (silence) "Well, I think I'd better be going. I'll let you get back to your work—good luck!"

Avoid Diminishing

When we diminish, we witness another person's emotion and willfully reflect it back to them much smaller than it really is. We do this because of our emotional response, not theirs: We might sincerely wish their experience was less awful, or we think we can help by staying optimistic and drawing attention to the upsides. But this instinct can backfire since from the other person's perspective, it sounds like, "You have no right to feel how you do," or even, "Your perception is wrong, i.e., you are wrong."

Examples:

A: "It was a really traumatic birth, and I don't think I'm quite over it yet."

B: "Well, be glad you only had the one. My neighbor had triplets!"

A: "I'm beginning to seriously wonder how we're going to survive the next few months financially..."

B: "Don't be silly, you'll be fine. You have a roof over your head and food on the table; that's more than some."

A: "I'm devastated. I don't know how I can go on."

B: "You poor thing! You've had a little break up, that's all. We've all been there. You'll get through it."

Avoid Dismissing

It can take a lot of bravery and trust to open up to someone, and most people willfully keep quiet about things if they think they don't warrant any attention. So, if someone shares something personal with you, it is a big deal, end of story. When we dismiss, we are essentially saying, "This doesn't matter," and throwing that person's courage back in their face. Again, we can do this sometimes because we have good intentions and want to downplay the hurt or hurry along to find a solution without hearing the emotional content being shared.

Examples:

A: "I've had it. I'm cutting all of them out of my life forever, I'm serious!"

B: "Just calm down, okay?"

A: "So now I'm really wondering if I can trust her at all. Has my whole marriage to her been a lie?"

B: "Come on, I think you're exaggerating a bit there."

A: "I just want to die."

B: "Oh, is it that time of the month again?"

Avoid Leading Questions

Remember that empathic listening is non-judgmental and non-directional. But if you ask a leading question, it's deliberately pushing the conversation in the direction you want it to go, i.e., asking a question with a clear idea of what you'd like the answer to be. This puts the other person in a spot, telling them how they're *supposed* to feel . . . while ignoring how they actually do.

A: "It's been such a difficult time for us all."

B: "But you're doing better now, right?"

A: "I've never been angrier at a person in my life."

B: "What do you think it would take to forgive him?"

A: "I miss her every day."

B: "It's been quite a long time now, hasn't it?"

Avoid Advice or Personal Anecdotes

Responding to a person's statement about themselves with a personal anecdote is just a way to say, "That's nice . . . but let's talk about me!" It may feel like a useful interjection, and in your mind, you may well wish to point out the connection or the shared experience, but in almost all cases, the other person is not interested in what someone else has felt or done—they are immersed in *their* experience.

Likewise, giving advice can create distance because it sets you above them as an all-knowing expert. What's more, when a person shares their emotions with you, they primarily want to be seen and heard, not fixed.

A: "And then she said she wanted to spend some time apart! Can you believe it?!"

B: "I remember when your mother and I were having troubles back in the day . . ."

A: ". . . and we've been really struggling with everyone's health this year. It seems like we are all run down and completely exhausted . . ."

B: "Zinc. You've got to supplement with zinc, trust me. It's the best immune support. Plus, I've been drinking this nettle tea every day, and I haven't had a cold for ages."

A: "This is the second time I've been in the bottom third of the class, and it's really starting to get to me. What if I'm actually not cut out for any of this?"

B: "I think you should speak to a careers counselor."

As you can see, in each of the above examples, there is a major empathy fail because Speaker B has not managed to see, hear, and reflect back Speaker A's emotional reality. Either they dismiss or diminish it, or they invalidate it by trying to lead the conversation elsewhere or insert their own opinions and advice.

Well, so much for what *not* to do. Let's look at how to provide empathic statements, and exactly what to say.

Acknowledge Their Courage

"Thank you for sharing this with me. I'm glad you trust me enough to confide in me."

"I know it's not easy to talk about this stuff . . . but I'm so glad you did."

"Well, you spoke up, and that took courage. You should be proud of yourself!"

Ask Empathic Questions

As we explored in a previous section, ask questions with the intention of understanding more and gaining clarity rather than leading or inserting your own judgments and opinions.

"How do you feel about all this?"

"Can you tell me more about X?"

"I want to understand—why did X happen?"

You can also use emotion labels to ask questions that not only clarify but reflect and ask the other person if you're properly hearing them.

"You say XYZ, and I wonder if that means you're feeling very ABC. Have I understood that right?"

Compliment Their Character

When someone is distressed, they may feel overwhelmed, confused, or seriously doubtful of their own worth and abilities. They may also worry about how they're coping and may carry some shame about how they feel. If you can confirm to them that they do indeed possess positive characteristics and that they're doing just fine, you can offer an enormous sense of encouragement and relief. Importantly, this is not just saying, "Don't worry! You'll be fine!" It's more about realistically recognizing how they're coping in the here and now, and that you have faith in them.

"Well, this has certainly been a very difficult situation, but I think you've handled it with a lot of strength and courage."

"It's not been easy, but I'm impressed with your perseverance."

"I think you're doing such a good job of handling things right now."

Show You Care

The simplest and most obvious statements you can make!

"I'm here for you. Any time you need to talk, just get in touch."

"What can I do to help?"

"We're all on your side, and we care so much about you."

Offering empathic statements may feel a little awkward at first, but the more you practice, the easier it gets. Just remember that you need to stay sincere, be authentic, and let your words come from a genuine place of interest in the other person's emotional world.

An Empathic Statement Formula

Stay attentive and curious. During an empathic conversation, of course you want to react naturally in the moment, but it doesn't hurt to have a rough guide to structure your statements so that you're sure you're covering all the bases. The following step-by-step process can be a great starting point, but you'll want to tweak it depending on the circumstances.

Step 1:

Use short words and phrases to signal encouragement and attention (obviously, adjust the expressions to fit your own context and choose what fits naturally!).

"Wow!"

"Hmmm."

"Uh huh."

"Oh my God."

"Yikes!"

Step 2:

Show your identification with a phrase that acknowledges and labels the emotional content being shared with you.

"That must be . . . (really disappointing/strange/a tricky situation)."

"That is . . . (unfortunate/stressful/outrageous)."

"It can be so . . . (heartbreaking to lose a pet/frustrating when you get ill/hard when relatives push boundaries)."

"It's hard to . . . (deal with loss/stay calm at a time like this/ask for help)."

"What a . . . (shame/tough time you've had/challenge)."

As before, try to avoid diagnosing the problem, passing judgment, or putting words in the other person's mouth. Use close synonyms, and be careful about making assumptions (for example, "You must be devastated," when the person hasn't expressed anything to suggest that's what they feel).

Remember the emotion wheel and, if it's possible, try to match the intensity of certain emotions to mirror what the person is sharing with you. If, for example, the person is mildly irritated, notice this and reflect it by saying, "It can be so annoying dealing with airline companies," rather than, "You must be so enraged right now!" Observe and notice the words they are using, and then reflect back with an emotion word that indicates the intensity, or else use terms like "a little," "somewhat," or "kind of" to check in with just how much of this emotion they're actually experiencing.

Step 3:

Finish with either:

- a small detail to show that you were paying attention
- a question to invite them to direct the conversation as they see fit
- or an action/suggested action to bring the conversation to a conclusion

For example:

- "Wow. That must be such a weird position to be in. To realize that you have so much in common with your boyfriend's ex—right down to the same name spelt the same way! It's one L in your name, right? I know that's not a common spelling, which is what makes it even more bizarre..."
- "Unbelievable. What an unfair thing for your brother to have said to you. What do you think you're going to do now?"
- "Gosh, I'm so sorry to hear all this. Would it help if I gave you a call tomorrow at

around three just to see how you're doing?"

The other person will let you know when they're ready to let the conversation come to a close, but you play your part by summarizing what you've heard (summarizing is just another form of reflecting) and either offering an action or suggesting a possible action they can take (remembering not to give advice).

Actions always speak louder than words. If someone says, "To be frank, I'm feeling awful right now and I just want to be on my own," then the best way to communicate your empathy is to respect what they say and leave them alone. Words are cheap, but you may find yourself in a situation where your kind actions are worth more. Offer to give them a lift home, organize an appointment, make excuses for them at the party, give them a hug, or fetch your favorite ice cream from the corner store, for example.

In closing, here are a few other useful statements you might like to use, depending on the situation at hand.

"It sounds as though you did everything you could."

"I can see that this hasn't been easy for you."

"You're holding up really well considering what you've been dealing with."

"If it were me, I'd feel exactly the same way!"

"I hear you."

"That makes sense."

"I'm sure I can't understand exactly what you're going through, but I am here, and I am listening."

"In your position, anyone would do the same."

"It's no wonder you feel this way."

"I think I'm beginning to understand . . ."

One thing not to say? "I know how you feel." It might be true, but nobody wants to hear it, and no matter how sincere you may be, it is an overused phrase that will only come across as trite.

Nonviolent Communication/NVC

All throughout the book so far, we have focused on how to *have* more empathy: read fiction, acknowledge your own biases, and learn to really listen and reflect with curiosity when people share their stories with you. However, empathy is not just a passive state of mind we adopt, but also a guiding principle behind everything we do. In this section, we'll be looking at **how to take our newly developed capacity for empathy and test-drive it in the**

place where it's most needed: conflict. It is during the spontaneous back-and-forth between two people of different perspectives that we realize we don't just need to *have* empathy, but to *show* it.

When you communicate with empathy, everything changes. In this chapter, we'll explore the fascinating world of nonviolent communication (hereafter NVC), which is a model and theory of human communication first introduced by social worker and therapist Dr. Marshall Rosenberg. Using the techniques we'll explore below, Dr. Rosenberg helped mitigate conflict-ridden discussions in war-torn countries like Serbia and Rwanda and all over the Middle East. According to him, NVC is a way to peacefully and respectfully communicate our own needs whilst having enough empathy and compassion for the needs of those we're communicating with.

Rosenberg believed that we are all capable of empathy . . . but that we don't always know the best strategy for expressing it! In fact, even when we intend to be compassionate and understanding, we may still communicate "violently" because we don't know any better. As you read, you'll probably notice how many of the approaches/techniques align well with the principles of listening, reflecting, and perspective-taking we identified above.

It is one thing to empathically listen as another person shares their emotions with you, but quite another when *you* also have emotions, and they are interacting in difficult ways with another person's. This is where we need a skill above and beyond empathy—we need to understand our perspective, their perspective, and **how the two are going to harmoniously cooperate with one another.**

To use NVC, we must always remember to:

- Be mindful and responsible in the way we use words to communicate our needs
- Constantly try to establish and maintain contact with the other person—our main goal is connection and understanding, *not* to assert, dominate, or "win"
- Seek to first understand but also make yourself understood
- Stay alert in case you slip into conflictual language again

The NVC model is simple and contains four components/steps:

1. Observations
2. Feelings
3. Needs
4. Requests

Observations

The first major step, and one often overlooked, is to **objectively become aware of the facts of the situation—and separate them out from interpretations, assumptions, and judgments about those facts**. This seems simple on the surface but can be tricky in real life.

Can you describe, with complete neutrality, what is happening or what has happened? What would a neutral third-party observer see if they were filming the situation with a camera?

We start with a neutral observing step so that we can orient both parties of the conversation in the same universe, seeking the common ground they both stand on. If you lead immediately with your own perspective (even if it's not "violent" per se), you are triggering a defensive reaction in the other person, and connection is lost. You don't necessarily have to agree on *everything* at the very outset, but you need to settle on a few basic shared facts before proceeding.

Here's an example. You're on vacation abroad visiting a new place with your partner, who is complaining bitterly about everything from the food to the weather to the crowds. You're getting frustrated.

A neutral observation might be: "We've tried six restaurants in a row and you didn't want to eat at any of them. It's too late now to get lunch, and we're both hungry."

Another might be: "You haven't liked any of the new food we've tried since arriving here."

However, it is less of an observation and more of a judgment or interpretation if we say, "I'm sick of how difficult you're being. I don't know why you want to ruin this vacation for us," or, "Why are you such a stick-in-the-mud? You never, ever want to try anything new!"

The best way to test whether your observations are truly neutral is to ask whether the other person would agree with them.

Feelings

Of course, we all have our own unique take on the objective event that unfolded. Here, **consider what you and the other person are feeling.** Just as we did with the emotion wheel, try to name the feeling as well as locate it on the body, and understand its intensity and direction.

According to Rosenberg, *all feelings arise in connection with our needs, met or unmet.* In fact, a big part of the reason we communicate at all is because we are seeking, in one way or another, to have our needs met. Therefore, if we want to communicate effectively, we need to understand the needs hidden beneath every emotion, and everything expressed in communication.

Again, this is not always easy. It is very tempting, for example, to confuse how we feel with how we think we should feel, or what we believe others are making us feel. We need to be extra careful that in expressing our feelings, we are not implicating someone else or interpreting their behavior. At the same time, we can't be confused about other people's feelings and mistake them for our own. We need to take responsibility for our own feelings . . . and only our own feelings. Rosenberg cautions against "false feelings" that wrongly implicate the other person.

For example:

"I feel that nothing I suggest is ever good enough for you."

"I feel put on the spot."

"I feel that you're being unfair."

Just because something follows the words "I feel" doesn't mean it's a genuine feeling. In the above cases, the other person is very likely to hear an attack—the "feelings" are positioning them as unpleasable, unfair, or doing something to put the other person on the spot. Can you imagine anyone agreeing with this? Again, it only creates resistance. The goal is to express how you feel without making it about the other person. In other words, don't package up your own feelings with value judgments, blame, or interpretations about the other person. Instead, for example, you could say:

"I'm so frustrated."

"I feel really disappointed."

"I feel angry."

When it comes to this step of the process, keep things short and sweet and focus solely on what you feel. Can you put it in one or two words only?

Needs

After you've touched base with shared objective facts and then expressed how you feel, it's time to consider the needs of everyone in the situation.

What are your needs here? Are they being met or not?

What are the needs of the other person? Are they being met or not?

Sometimes, it can be tricky to identify concrete needs; it may be easier to think in terms of what is important to each person and what they hold valuable. A need could be something simple (like the need for privacy or the need for help with a specific task), or it can be more general (the need to feel appreciated, or the need to feel that one's contribution is valued by the group). Often, there is a mix of big and small needs motivating us in any situation—it may take a conflict to show us what we never thought of as a need before!

Importantly, every human being shares a basic need in conversation for empathic connection, for social harmony, for validation, and for healing contact with those around us. So, even if it is not very clear what needs are going unmet, it is a safe assumption that in all cases, people are driven to connect, be seen, and find harmonious solutions.

Another important point is that **we shouldn't confuse needs with strategies to meet those needs**. For example, someone might have a need for a feeling of routine, predictability, and structure. This need may be going unmet because their workplace is chaotic and stressful. To try to meet their needs anyway, they become anxious perfectionists, trying to micromanage every detail and create a little order. It would be a mistake, however, to say that this person has a "need for perfection." The perfectionism is just a strategy (that may, incidentally, not be working all that well!). The deeper need is for routine and structure.

When we communicate, we need to address the need beneath the feeling. If we only engage with the strategy, we are dealing with a superficiality and will not reach a genuine resolution to any conflict. How do you know what is a strategy and what is a need? The big clue is this: needs are universal, and strategies are not; strategies tend to be more specific and situation dependent. Every human being has some degree of need for routine and structure in life; not every human being needs perfectionism.

During this step, you express your needs in relation to the feeling you identified in the previous step. If you felt frustrated, you could say, "I feel frustrated because I have a need to eat lunch at a certain time or I get lightheaded and grumpy," or, "I feel disappointed because it's important to me that I make the best of my vacation time and enjoy myself. Having a good time also makes me feel like our relationship is solid and that we're happy." Again, we need to guard against allowing judgment or interpretation to sneak in: "I need you to be less indecisive."

Requests

Finally, given that we have communicated our perception of the situation, our feelings about it, and what we need, now comes the part where we ask that those needs are met. This is, of course, a big part of why we communicate in the first place—we are trying to create some kind of change in the world that would support our needs. But this is an important step because it's the first time we deliberately ask that someone accommodate our needs.

A request is not a demand or an obligation for the other person. You may have expressed yourself perfectly and have a valid claim, but it is still just a request—which means it can be turned down. In the final step, ask for something concrete that speaks to all three of the previous steps. For example, "I'd like to go back to that restaurant we just passed by and have lunch there," or, "I need a little time to cool off. Perhaps we can spend tomorrow exploring the city on our own and meet up again on Thursday."

Importantly, **we take responsibility for meeting our own needs**. It is up to us to know what we want and need and to share that clearly, without expecting others to mindread. A request is an invitation for someone else to help you meet your clearly identified need. That may be by doing something concrete themselves or allowing you to do something concrete. These requests are best when given as simple, concrete actions that a person can take immediately, and framed as something you want rather than something you don't want (although it may be necessary to sometimes set a boundary or say no in this way).

A request can begin with words like, *could you, can you, please*, or variations on *I'd like it if . . .* Framing things as a question communicates that you are asking, not telling.

Avoid requests that are:

- Too vague ("Can you be less difficult?")
- Impossible to fulfil ("I really want that closed restaurant to be open right now.")
- Framed as what you don't want rather than what you want ("Please stop whining.")
- Framed as demands or even threats ("Just stop talking or I swear I'm walking away.")

You might be wondering, *what if the other person refuses the request?* Well, it's a possibility. However, you will know that *you* have done everything in your power to communicate clearly and respectfully. When faced with someone's unwillingness to help you meet reasonable needs, you must make a decision. Human beings are interconnected, and we all lean on one another in order to get our universal needs met. That said, we are all responsible as individuals for meeting our own needs as far as possible.

It is my responsibility to ask for what I need.

It is *not* my responsibility to decide what the other person's response to these requests is.

It is my responsibility to find people and situations that meet my needs—and move away from circumstances that continually undermine my ability to have these needs met.

Once you speak up while on your vacation, the other person may hear you and respond positively, agreeing to take actions that will meet your needs (because they care about you, after all!). On the other hand, they may refuse to do so. If this happens repeatedly, you may decide that you are unwilling to have a relationship with someone who is expressly uninterested in meeting your reasonable requests.

Either way, you have diffused conflict and moved the situation to a workable resolution. None of this is possible without empathy. In NVC, you always have a choice, and you can always allow empathy to guide you in this way.

When the Shoe Is on the Other Foot

Respect, as they say, is a two-way street. We can communicate our own feelings and needs with empathy and understanding. But the other side of this skill is to hear other people's requests with the same empathy and understanding.

In NVC, we **express honestly**, but we also **receive empathically**.

Obviously, few people are going to be well-versed in Rosenberg's NVC techniques. So, we have to give people the benefit of the doubt and work with what we have. If in a conflict someone is upset or not making much sense, we can take the initiative and encourage them to express themselves along the four components as described above.

We can start by focusing them on the shared, neutral common ground. State your own observations as best as you can and make a point of checking in with them to signal your willingness to find a shared starting point. "Have I got that right?" or, "Would you agree with that?"

If they share some facts that are mixed up with emotional interpretations and distortions, take the time to model a non-judgmental perspective and reflect back to them only those parts of their expression that are genuinely factual.

"You were totally rude to show up at the time you did."

"Okay, I hear you. So we can agree that I arrived too late."

Once you've established some common ground, take the lead by sharing your own feelings and then inviting them to do the same—and listen to what they say. Here, the emotion wheel can help, and if it's appropriate, you could focus the conversation by offering tentative labels. "It seems like this has made you pretty angry," or, "I'd like to understand what's going on with you right now—can you tell me how you're feeling?"

Do the same when it comes to needs. Even when people are hurt or upset, you may be surprised at how ready they are to follow suit if you can take the lead and model a focus on needs rather than placing blame. You could also ask them outright, "What do you need right now?" You may need to pry a little (use that magical word "why") and use your powers of genuine curiosity to get to the root of what they're really needing in this conflict. Naturally, you will need to suspend your own ego for a time—especially if what they're expressing makes you feel guilty or uncomfortable.

Finally, remember that the conversation is not just about you getting your needs met, but about them getting theirs met, too. You can combine these—for example, "I think moving forward I would like to start these meetings a lot later in the afternoons so I can get to them more promptly. Do you think that's something you could do? Or is there something else you'd like to try?"

As you talk, you can't go wrong with deliberately and frequently signaling your intention to meet both your needs, to connect harmoniously, and to understand them while being understood yourself:

"I'm on your side."

"Please help me understand . . ."

"I'd like to figure this out."

"Can we find a solution that works for us both?"

"Please help me understand all this from your point of view."

"I'm listening."

Finally, one key skill: gracefully accepting a "no." If you respectfully make a reasonable request, and someone respectfully and reasonably denies it, then there is nothing to do but accept it. Do not get angry or upset. Sometimes, the most empathic thing we can do for someone is believe them when they tell us *no*.

How to Be Assertive AND Empathic

So, the eternal balance is between expressing our own needs whilst taking account of other peoples'. Is it really possible to be kind and understanding to others while also asserting our boundaries and getting our needs met? The answer is absolutely yes!

Not only can we be assertive while maintaining empathy, our assertiveness may in fact be "boosted" when combined with empathy. Being able to truly understand other people's perspectives can mean we are actually *more* effective at asserting our rights and boundaries—all while maintaining connection and harmony with them.

You might find yourself with two conflicting needs: the need to protect your time, your resources, or your energy on one hand, but the need to please others, to stay connected to the group, and to "not rock the boat" on the other. You'll need tact, warmth, and a little diplomacy to pull it off—in other words, you'll need empathy.

Use Simple Empathic Assertions

Remember that "assertiveness" is not about being rude, aggressive, hostile, or forceful. Think of it more in terms of being direct and honest and standing up for your rights. We *all* need to be assertive at some point or another, and asserting ourselves is not the same as conflict. Many people who are compassionate and empathic struggle with self-empathy and boundaries precisely because deep down they misunderstand assertiveness and their right to claim it.

We are assertive when we maintain our own rights while respecting others'. Most of us know that bullying, blaming, and shaming are not part of being assertive, but then again, neither is being passive-aggressive, guilt-tripping people, or being curt and cold.

An empathic assertion contains two parts. The first part is your considerate acknowledgement of the other person's position, and the second is where you assert your own position. By putting both these parts together, you are demonstrating that your empathy and understanding for them is *not* in conflict with you asserting your own needs or boundaries.

For example:

"I know that it's not what you want to hear, but I can't help you out this time."

"I can see that it's not convenient, but I can't agree to be there."

"I can imagine that you're busy right now, but there's no way I can wait longer for the work."

"I'm really sorry, but no."

If you want to dial up the diplomacy, remove the word "but" entirely and simply present these two components as two sentences." This goes beyond politeness, though. People can get offended by a "no" if they feel that you don't quite understand how it affects them. If you first acknowledge that you do fully understand their position, they're a little more likely to respect your refusal. They will be more ready to accommodate you if they are aware that you have at least given some thought to their side of things.

Using the "Positive No"

You can probably see that these simple empathic assertions are not going to be enough for more complex situations or people whom you share a more serious relationship. The above examples are polite yet firm and are great for kindly asserting boundaries in the workplace or with acquaintances. For everyone else, you might need to use a "positive no." In fact, using a simple empathic assertion may put certain people on the defensive if they feel they are owed a little more. Here's how to do it.

1. Acknowledge the request and show gratitude for it. "Oh wow, thank you for thinking of me. I'm honored you thought to ask me for help!"

2. Next, move on to what is currently meaningful in your own life, including your priorities and focus (i.e., gently revealing what you will be doing instead of their request). "At the moment, I'm really focusing a lot on spending quality time with the family, especially after Madeleine's birth!"
3. Only then do you say no, but framed in such a way as to highlight that you cannot accommodate both the request and your own priorities. "Unfortunately, that means I don't have too much time on my hands for additional projects, so I can't help this time."
4. Close off the "positive no" with something helpful. Either make a suggestion, point them in the direction of someone who can help, or, if you can, suggest in what ways you might be able to say yes. At the very least, you can wish them well for whatever they're requesting. "Sorry about that, but now that I think of it, Emma has mentioned that she had some availability, so you could possibly ask her? Either way, I hope it works out—it sounds like such a great idea!"

In the above, you can see how the "no" is cushioned in many, many layers of warmth, consideration, and courtesy. You are doing several things with such a refusal:

- Communicating *no* clearly so there is no room for misunderstanding, guilt tripping, or negotiation
- Empathizing with the request-giver's position and delivering the refusal in a way that doesn't undermine your respect for them or make them wrong for asking
- Giving the person a peek into your own circumstances and reasoning so that they are invited to empathize with *you*

The mere fact of anybody saying no with this much tact and care is an enormous sign: "I care about this and about our connection. I care about not offending you even though I also need to assert this boundary and say no."

Try an Empathy Prompt

In psychologist Craig Malkin's book *Rethinking Narcissism*, he describes a technique for saying no that can actually soothe the narcissist in your life. You don't have to be dealing with an actual narcissist, though—the technique also works for anyone you suspect will be overly sensitive to criticism or rejection.

Step 1 is to start by emphasizing the value of the relationship between you both. This offers the other person validation and support, lessening the chances of them reacting in defensiveness.

"You know that you're one of my best friends in the world..."

"Jane, I value your opinion enormously..."

"You are hands down the most important person in my world right now..."

Step 2 is to describe the situation succinctly using the ABCD method (which is not unlike what we discussed earlier in the nonviolent communication section):

A is affect, i.e., your feelings

B is the behavior that you are unhappy with, or the thing you are saying no to

C is the consequences of this behavior

D is for describe what you want, i.e., make a request or say no

"I feel completely overwhelmed and stressed out (A) when you change our plans at the last minute (B), and it's beginning to make me feel like you don't care about the plans we make together (C). I'd like it if we could have a rule where we don't cancel something if it's less than twenty-four hours away."

This is an empathic, nonviolent way to be assertive. You don't set up a "me versus you" dynamic but instead make it "us versus the problem." This technique is also great when you feel that someone has already violated a boundary or ignored a reasonable no on your part. It's easy to say "no" to a simple request, but sometimes situations themselves place a demand on us, and we need to find a way to assertively resist them.

The "Soft Startup"

This technique comes to us from married marriage therapists Drs. John and Julie Gottman. It's useful for bringing up a concern, gripe, or issue but without it causing upset or starting a fight. According to the Gottmans, a "hard startup" is where we use accusatory language and lash out at our partners with "you" language:

"You make me so mad."

"You always do this."

"You're being so immature right now."

This is hard language because it comes across without any care or kindness. Instead, you need to lead confrontations with a lot more empathy, especially if it concerns someone very close to you, like a spouse.

Start by asking if someone actually has time to talk—don't just spring it on them. Then, "complain without blame" by beginning with terms like:

"Maybe you didn't realize that you were doing it, but earlier on . . ."

"I understand that it's been a difficult time lately, so this is not easy to bring up . . ."

"You know I absolutely love that you're so excited about the new puppy, but I've noticed that . . ."

Doing so cushions any conflict or criticism in a package of mostly kindness, warmth, and understanding. Something else to keep in mind is that things will be far easier if you are in a relaxed state when you bring up your issue or kindly refuse a request they're making. If you are bringing something to their attention, choose a time when you'll both be receptive and available, take plenty of deep breaths, and speak "low and slow"—all these things will send the unconscious message that you are not presenting a threat of any kind. If they bring up the issue and you're feeling defensive or upset, there's nothing wrong with pausing for a deep breath or even asking if you can step away and come back to the conversation later.

The Empathic Communication Toolkit for Handling Conflict

Empathic communication is not always easy, and it's seldom done perfectly. When there are delicate feelings involved and high stakes, it's normal to feel a little apprehensive or misunderstood. But the good news is that this kind of engagement gets better with practice. In fact, the more you bring this attitude to your closest relationships, the more you will indirectly *teach* others how to connect with you, and you might find with time that you both learn a few good habits along the way.

Here are some conversational tools to stock your "empathic communication toolkit" with, along with some concrete examples for what that looks like out in the wild. None of these are one-size-fits-all, however—as always, use a little common sense and think carefully about the unique person in front of you and what the social context you're both inhabiting demands.

Open-Ended Questions

When in doubt, ask a question. Take a step back and release tension, putting them in the driver's seat for a while. If you feel some resistance from the other person, pause, put your guard down, and lead with curiosity and respect.

"Oh, what would you know about it!"

"Well, perhaps I don't quite understand. But I'm listening now. What am I not yet seeing? Tell me."

Any time you are in an argument or an emotionally difficult conversation, use open-ended questions to signal your willingness to remove your own judgment from the equation—while still asking for what you need. This will keep you both empathic and assertive. At the same time, you are telling people that even though you are saying no or bringing up an issue with them, you are *still* interested in their perspective and are still available to listen and empathize.

"As I said, there's not much I can do about my work schedule, so it's a no from me. But can I ask, why has it been so hard to get reliable babysitters?"

Zoom in on Strengths, not Deficits

Both yours and the other person's, and in the situation as a whole. When you say no, make a complaint, or bring up an issue, people may accurately or inaccurately hear the hidden message, "Something is wrong here; something is lacking." If you focus instead on what is *right* with the situation, you counter this impulse to hear criticism or rejection—which only causes people to shut down.

Consciously choose to recognize the positives. Even if you are raising a legitimate complaint, nobody is misguided in every area of life, and even if you are correcting their harmful behavior or asking for an apology, try to remember that this person also has positive qualities. Very few people *intend* consistently to do wrong, and nobody wants to feel incompetent, evil, lazy, reckless, or untrustworthy.

Use empathy to imagine what they most like about themselves, and try to acknowledge that even in the midst of conflict. "Look, I've always admired how much you clearly care about your kids, but little Johnny's behavior is really unacceptable..."

Let Them Go First

It's not just polite to ask people's feelings before expressing your own, it shows empathy. Let's say you wanted to bring to someone's attention the fact that their comments during a meeting were inappropriate. You could use a "soft startup" approach and begin by asking what they thought and felt. "I wanted to have a quick chat about what you said in the meeting earlier today—I think you probably know the comment I'm referring to! I just wanted to properly understand what you meant. Could you clue me in on what you were trying to say?"

It may be that after one further explanation, you realize that you've misunderstood the comment, and the conflict is gone. Or, if there really is reason for hurt feelings, they are far more likely to hear them since you went out of your way to give them the floor and listen to their side of things *first*.

__Language that Normalizes__

What can put people on edge is simply the recognition that someone else is unhappy, that there is a conflict, or even that they are in line to receive criticism or complaints. It's a Big Problem. But there is a way to communicate in which you *don't* pathologize the other person or imbue the whole situation with shame and a sense of catastrophe.

It's a good idea, even during conflict, to remind people that they are not alone and that there is not something uniquely bad or wrong about them—even if the current situation is difficult. In terms of being assertive and empathic, this means saying things like:

"Do you think you could wash up the dishes when you're done? I've noticed a few times that the kitchen's been a mess afterward. I know, I know, I'm totally lazy when it comes to cleaning up after myself, and I sometimes need a reminder, too!"

"It's okay. I know that when people are stressed, they often can't help lashing out at those closest to them."

"I get it. That was a perfectly understandable response."

__Conciliatory Body Language__

Just because you're being assertive, saying no, or having an uncomfortable conversation, it doesn't mean you can't continue to express empathy and a spirit of cooperation. Try to stay mindful and maintain eye contact, smile (if appropriate), maintain a warm and relaxed tone of voice, and keep an open body. Scan your posture for areas of tightness (an automatic and unconscious reflection of fight-or-flight being activated) and choose to soften and open instead. Uncross arms and legs, unclench your face muscles, and use gestures that emphasize open and extended hands.

Summary

- In empathic communication, we should always seek to understand first and to create connection. Empathic statements can help, but avoid deflecting, diminishing, dismissing, dominating the conversation with leading questions, or giving advice or personal anecdotes. Instead, ask empathic questions, compliment something in their character, or do something practical to show you care.
- The nonviolent communication model consists of four components: observations, feelings, needs, and requests. First, become aware of the objective facts of the situation and separate them out from interpretations, assumptions, and judgments about those facts. Next, share what you are feeling,

remembering that feelings are connected to our needs, met or unmet.
- Then, express these needs without blaming and without confusing needs with strategies used to meet those needs. Finally, finish with a request for that need to be met. Avoid requests that are vague, impossible to fulfil, framed as what you don't want, or framed as a demand that can't be refused. A request does not entitle us to receive what we ask for, so we should graciously accept if it isn't granted.
- To be both assertive and empathic, use techniques like the "positive no" or the "soft startup" when setting a boundary.
- When managing conflicts or difficult communication, remember to use open-ended questions; focus on strengths; let the other person lead; normalize rather than pathologize; and use open, conciliatory body language to show that you are on the same side.

Summary Guide

CHAPTER 1: UNDERSTANDING EMPATHY

- Empathy is about the ability to take another person's perspective. It is similar to "theory of mind," which is the human capacity to understand another person's state of mind and comprehend that it is totally different from our own. Empathy is not only theory of mind but "theory of heart"—to *feel* other people's emotions—and it's hardwired into our brains and bodies.
- Empathy is not about any particular *situation*, but about a unique individual's *perspective* on that situation.
- Though it is an innate human ability, it is in decline. We need to consciously cultivate and develop empathy.
- There are three kinds of empathy: Cognitive empathy is empathy based on knowing or understanding what someone else is going through, on an intellectual level.
- Emotional empathy is the ability to actually share and take some part in the emotional experience of another person.
- With compassionate empathy, we put our feelings of understanding and sympathy to good use. We try to resolve problems,

remove burdens, or inspire insights that will help progress the situation.
- In an empathic interaction, move from cognitive to emotional to compassionate empathy.

CHAPTER 2: FLEX YOUR EMPATHY MUSCLES

- Reading literature may actually make you a more empathic human being. It can reduce bias and prejudice and literally change your brain physiology. The key is in the ability to switch perspectives.
- Choose literary fiction, preferably written in first person. Try authors who are different from yourself, or books about characters that are unlike yourself.
- Read actively and engage with the story. Pause to ask questions to investigate the character's point of view, switching perspectives and exploring motivations and desires. Ask yourself, "What does the human experience feel like for *this* specific human? Why?" Instead of asking how you would feel in their shoes, ask how *they* feel in their shoes. However, be discerning about what kind of perspectives you delve into!

- Another way to build empathy is to create "emotional literacy." Emotional literacy is the ability to identify and verbalize complex emotions. It is an act of self-awareness. With greater emotional identification and awareness comes more clarity, insight, and mastery—and better empathy.
- The emotion wheel is a helpful tool that helps you develop increased self-awareness, empathic mastery, and precision when it comes to emotions. It outlines shades and nuances of the eight primary emotions: sadness, anger, disgust, joy, trust, fear, surprise, and anticipation.

CHAPTER 3: MASTERING EMPATHY BASICS

- Your perspective on life is what makes you unique, but it can also be a source of isolation, misunderstanding, and conflict.
- A pre-conceived notion about who another person is may be the single biggest obstacle on the path to genuine empathy for them. Getting rid of bias is about more than guarding against sexism or racism and more about consciously choosing to remember that all people are united in their shared humanity.

- Prejudice is pre-judging what another's experience is and what it means. Stereotypes and categories undermine authentic connections with others. Bias is a filter through which all the information we receive about that person is distorted. Being empathic is not just about being kind. It's about clear, accurate perception and genuine comprehension of another worldview.
- To tackle your own prejudice, first acknowledge that you do have it! Consciously choose to expose yourself to the unfamiliar and challenge yourself to empathize not just with similarity but with difference. Assume there is always a common ground between you and another individual and actively choose to focus on that instead of what is different.
- Forget the Golden Rule and remember that the very meaning of compassion, kindness, and empathy changes depending on the recipient. Show people compassion, but on *their* terms, not yours.
- In interactions, try to explore: what the other person thinks about themselves, what the other person thinks about you, what you think about them, and what you think about yourself. This can be especially helpful during a conflict.

CHAPTER 4: LISTENING IS EMPATHY IN ACTION

- To listen effectively and empathically, we need to let our egos take a back seat so the other person can lead. If we are sensitive, alert, and respectful, we can listen without an agenda.
- Listen with maximum attention without getting distracted by anything other than the perspective being shared with you in that very moment.
- Seek to understand, not to judge, appraise, or evaluate—in fact, your opinion is irrelevant! Only your presence and awareness are necessary. Have radical acceptance for what is simply because it is.
- Maintain deep curiosity. Ask questions that create space in which the other person can expand. This sends the message, "You are important. How you are feeling has value. I am listening because what you are going through is worthy of attention and worth knowing more about."
- Use mirroring, paraphrasing, or reflecting to show active listening.
- Body language can be empathic too, and when your body mirrors another person's, this is a way to show physical "active listening" of the body.

- To show that your body is listening, face the person, make comfortable eye contact, and seek to concur with "yeses" or head nods. Then mirror their words, voice, posture, or other idiosyncrasies.
- When mirroring, be mindful of the gender or cultural context, and only reflect what is positive. Avoid mirroring strong negative emotions (panic, anger, depression) and instead model a sense of calm by slowing down and taking a deep breath; the other person may then mirror you.

CHAPTER 5: EMPATHY IS A MINDSET SHIFT

- When we listen empathically and reflect, we go quiet and still within ourselves so we can receive as accurate a picture of the other person's account as possible. We use mirroring and paraphrasing without questioning, leading, or starting a new thread.
- We can reflect either content, feeling, or meaning, but should always remain non-directional and non-judgmental.
- Avoid psychologizing. When we interpret people's experiences, we are no longer fully listening to them.

- Empathy is impossible without curiosity. Curiosity is about more than asking questions—it's about having a sincere desire to understand someone else's heart, mind, and complete experience. It requires imagination, a hunger to learn, and an open mind.
- The main thing that gets in the way of real curiosity in empathic listening is the impulse to insert our own opinion, perspective, or frame of reference into the conversation. Imagine that learning to be interested in others is not a boring challenge, but a gift and an opportunity.
- There are three kinds of curiosity: diversive (interest in novelty), epistemic (deeper inquiry into knowledge itself), and empathic. Whenever you notice mild interest in novelty, see if you can explore and amplify it till it becomes richer empathic curiosity.
- Keep the spark of curiosity alive by consistently asking why, digging beneath the superficiality of a situation, and challenging yourself to see nothing as boring.
- Random acts of kindness can make us more empathic. Try to be more alert to other people's needs and respond spontaneously to them.
- Kindness is a shift from focus on the self to focus on the other. Continually ask yourself, "How are other people doing? What do they need?"

CHAPTER 6: EMPATHIC COMMUNICATION

- In empathic communication, we should always seek to understand first and to create connection. Empathic statements can help, but avoid deflecting, diminishing, dismissing, dominating the conversation with leading questions, or giving advice or personal anecdotes. Instead, ask empathic questions, compliment something in their character, or do something practical to show you care.
- The nonviolent communication model consists of four components: observations, feelings, needs, and requests. First, become aware of the objective facts of the situation and separate them out from interpretations, assumptions, and judgments about those facts. Next, share what you are feeling, remembering that feelings are connected to our needs, met or unmet.
- Then, express these needs without blaming and without confusing needs with strategies used to meet those needs. Finally, finish with a request for that need to be met. Avoid requests that are vague, impossible to fulfil, framed as what you don't want, or framed as a demand that can't be refused. A request does not entitle us to receive what we ask

for, so we should graciously accept if it isn't granted.
- To be both assertive and empathic, use techniques like the "positive no" or the "soft startup" when setting a boundary.
- When managing conflicts or difficult communication, remember to use open-ended questions; focus on strengths; let the other person lead; normalize rather than pathologize; and use open, conciliatory body language to show that you are on the same side.

www.ingramcontent.com/pod-product-compliance
Lightning Source LLC
Chambersburg PA
CBHW020529080526
44583CB00013B/788